AS DARK AS IT GETS

GETS

From Chains to Grace

by

Laura W. Dunavent MS, BSN, RN

My Story

ACKNOWLEDGEMENT:

I would like to thank Dr. Kinney who worked diligently to get my book published!

DEDICATION:

I dedicate the book to Dr. Guy Kinney, Elizabeth Hedlund, my son, and The mentoring team at Parker Publishers.

I pray for all of those who have suffered at the hands of loved ones.

TABLE OF CONTENTS

CHAPTER 1

THE DAY EVERYTHING CHANGED

November 5, 1988, began as a glorious and beautiful fall day in South Florida. I had recently married for the second time. My new husband, Jack, and I went to the Galleria Mall to do some Christmas shopping. The Galleria Mall is one of the most glamorous malls in Ft. Lauderdale. Especially during the holidays, it is so beautifully decorated, one cannot help but be moved by a feeling of Christmas joy.

I was in a great mood that day—probably one of the best moods I had been in for a very long time. Being a newlywed, and it being Christmas, there was a sense of peace I hadn't felt in years. For the first time in a long while, I was going to have a completely family-oriented

Christmas.

Family meant everything to me. I had been divorced for nine years and had raised my son, Joshua, by myself since he was just eighteen months old. Now, he was eight.

Being a single mother was not easy, and it hurt me deeply when my son would ask why he didn't have a daddy. I would try to reassure him that not having a daddy around was a real loss—a painful truth—but that we would be all right. My son never quite believed me. He felt left out, especially when he heard other kids talk about their dads and the things they did together. Those conversations always seemed to weigh on him in ways his little heart couldn't explain.

But now, my son had a father. And I had a family that resembled some kind of normalcy—a picture of what I thought life was supposed to look like. Or so I believed.

My husband, Jack, and I shopped all morning. We just had such a great time choosing gifts for all of our family and friends. **The gifts we picked out felt extra special—

**nicer in comparison to what I had purchased in prior years, because my budget, as a single mother, had always been tight. Being able to give more freely this year felt like a little piece of heaven.

After shopping for hours, Jack and I decided to have lunch. For the first time in my life, I ordered a Bloody Mary because I felt festive and happy, and the celebration just seemed to feel right. Jack and I laughed, joked, smiled, and behaved like newlyweds. We were having a wonderful time together. I truly believed that my life had taken a turn toward happiness. For the first time in what felt like forever, I was beginning to feel real joy—hopeful about a future I once thought I would never have.

I had peace of mind. I was feeling such joy and love because I believed I had married a man who loved me and my child. Jack and I had been married for six months, and I had no idea that this day would be our last day of enjoying our marriage.

After our wonderful shopping day at the mall, Jack and I arrived home around 5:00 p.m. That night, we had plans to go out with some friends, so Jack took a nap and I played a board game with Joshua.

Our babysitter, Donna, arrived at 8:00 p.m. as scheduled. The telephone rang while Joshua was answering the door and Jack was in the shower. My mother's second husband, Brian, was on the phone. I asked him playfully, "So, what do I owe for the pleasure of the telephone call?" But Brian didn't laugh. In a deep, quiet voice, heavy with sadness, he said, "Winnie..."—my family nickname—"are you sitting down?"

As I sat down slowly, already bracing myself for something bad, I tried to steady my voice enough to ask, "What's wrong, Brian?"

Immediately, I thought that something was wrong with my mother. Brian explained to me in a slow, methodical tone that my brother, Rodger, had been shot. I was shocked and dismayed at this news, but I replied, "Okay. I am a nurse and can surely nurse Rodger back to health. I have nursed everyone else's family members; I could certainly nurse one of my own family members." Then I had to ask the obvious question, "How badly hurt is Rodger?"

Brian just kept asking me to come to my parents' home right away before he told my mother about Rodger because he feared how she would react to the news. I asked again, "How bad is Rodger?" Brian just reiterated, "Come here now."

Feeling the desperation in my stepfather's voice, I started thinking about how I would juggle work and manage a lengthy stay in Kentucky to care for my brother. I was assuming that he was gravely injured and in the intensive care unit. Still, I was already making plans in my mind. Somehow, I would figure it all out—because I really wanted to nurse someone I loved. And I loved my brother. I felt like maybe this was the moment to show Rodger just how much he meant to me.

It had always been a deep disappointment to me that he hadn't come to my wedding. I knew he harbored resentments toward me, though I never fully understood why. Rodger had stopped speaking to me about four years ago. Maybe this would be the bridge back to our relationship. I thought maybe this tragedy could offer an opportunity for us to be close again. Not knowing the circumstances of why he had been shot was disturbing, but I tried to push those thoughts aside while preparing to leave for my mother's home.

My mother, Laura—whom I am named after—and her husband, Brian, lived about an hour and a half north of Ft. Lauderdale, in a city called Port St. Lucie. Jack was just getting out of the shower when I told him our evening plans had changed. I said we had to leave immediately for my mother's house because Rodger had been gravely injured. Brian was waiting for us to arrive so he could break the news to my mother. There was no time to lose.

Jack told the babysitter about our family emergency, and she agreed to stay with Joshua until we returned from Port St. Lucie. The telephone rang again. This time, it was my father's wife, Jean, calling from Kentucky. Jean informed me that my father was unable to speak to me due to his severe emotional state.

My father—whose name is John, or Johnny—often didn't make emotional or difficult phone calls himself. He would usually have Jean speak on his behalf and relay the conversation. So, for him not to come to the phone didn't seem particularly alarming. In fact, it was fairly normal. Not speaking on the phone was common among most of the men in our family.

Jack gently took the phone from my hand and said, "Let me handle this call." I listened attentively to his side of the conversation, trying to make sense of it. All I heard Jack say was, "Uh huh... yes... I understand."

I screamed, "Jack, is my brother dead?!"

He shook his head, signaling for me to wait until the call ended. But now I was feeling sick—completely over-taken by fear—and I could barely contain the panic bub-bling up inside of me. Tears started to fall as I cried out again, "Is Rodger dead? Just tell me!"

Jack put down the phone, and I saw the tears in his eyes. His hesitation terrified me. Then he said the words my brain couldn't fully process.

"Rodger is dead."

I collapsed to the floor, crying uncontrollably. Shock took over every part of me.

Jack said, "Please, Laura, there's more I need to tell

you. Please hold it together."

I screamed, "What?! What more could there possibly be?!"

He looked at me with heartbreak in his eyes and said, "Rodger shot himself."

"Oh my God! No! No! That cannot be true. He didn't shoot himself. He couldn't have!"

Jack said softly, "I'm so sorry, but according to the coroner, Rodger committed suicide."

The coroner's report later confirmed that Rodger had been depressed and had died from a self-inflicted gunshot wound to the chest. He died instantly..

In one's lifetime, there are only a few tragedies that can wreak havoc on your soul, cause brain damage, and hold enough power to alter the entire course of your life—and this was one of those tragedies. I cannot describe the cascade of emotions that come when a sibling commits suicide—especially a sibling who shared a history of abuse with you.

When Rodger and I were children, we made a pact. We promised each other that we would survive our childhood abuse, that we would stay close forever, and that we would become better people—and better parents—than our own had been. We clung to that dream. The loss of my brother was devastating.

After learning of Rodger's death, I remembered our pact, and I screamed out loud, "He promised me that we would survive!"

As I screamed, I dropped to my knees. A sharp, blinding pain tore through me—it felt like someone had taken a hot butcher knife, driven it deep into my abdomen, cut downward, and ripped out my internal organs. My brain felt like it had seized—I couldn't think. The room turned black. I couldn't hear anything, I couldn't speak.

I stayed on the floor, unmoving. No words, no purpose. Just staring. I was catatonic.

Later, I began to realize that the loss of my brother was

going to be nearly impossible for me to overcome. What made it harder was the unresolved pain. We hadn't spoken in over four years, and he left this world angry at me. I would never have the chance to tell him how much he meant to me—how deeply I loved him—or how sorry I was that I hadn't been emotionally healthy enough to truly enjoy having a brother.

Jack, lacking emotional maturity or experience, didn't know how to respond to my grief. His instinct was to numb it. He scrambled through our medicine cabinet and found a painkiller, which he insisted I take before we left for my mother's house in Port St. Lucie.

I didn't even know if my mother knew that Rodger had died.

I sat silently in the car on the way there—numb from shock, dulled by the narcotic, and consumed by a pain I didn't have words for. I wept quietly. My soul ached.

The drive to my mother's felt endless. But eventually, we arrived.

I took a deep breath and began to exit the car when I saw the front door of my mother's house open. My mother came running out toward the car. I got out, and we just embraced each other and cried. Our husbands went inside the house to begin preparing for the trip to Kentucky—to get everything in motion for the funeral.

All of us sat, cried, and tried to process the news as best—and as humanly—as possible, especially considering Rodger's death was neither an accident nor an act of God. It was deliberate. And it was sudden.

The travel arrangements were made quickly. The plan was that Jack, my mother, and I would fly from West Palm Beach to Nashville, Tennessee. The flight was scheduled for departure at 7:00 a.m.

It was around 10:00 p.m. when I found myself sitting quietly in the living room, trying to hold myself together. Suddenly, I remembered a dream I'd had just two days earlier—and the realization of it chilled me to my core.

In the dream, I was in Detroit, Michigan—a place I'd never been before—and I was frantic, trying to get my son on a bus to Nashville while I scrambled to catch a flight to Nashville myself. When I awoke, the dream had left me shaken. It was vivid, chaotic, and frightening.

Throughout my life, I had experienced terrible nightmares. I would often try to make sense of them and sometimes called my mother to help me interpret them using her dream book.

After dreaming about the flight to Nashville, I called her and told her about it. She asked me, "What does Detroit symbolize to you?"

Without hesitation, I said, "Violence."

And now, hearing our flight itinerary—flying to Nashville—I realized I had experienced a premonition. The dream had shown me something I hadn't understood at the time.

This was new for me. I'd never had a dream that fore-told anything. Most of my dreams were nonsense or night-mares with no clear meaning. But this one... this one had come true.

Two weeks later, the other part of the dream would come to pass—when I was preparing my son for his own travel to Kentucky. We arranged for Joshua to ride up with distant relatives who would arrive the day after we did.

Jack, my mother, and I drove from Port St. Lucie to Ft. Lauderdale to tell Joshua about Rodger and to get him ready for the funeral. I wasn't much help. My mind was shattered. But I did my best.

After getting Joshua ready for his trip, the three of us packed our things and left for the airport.

During the fifty-mile drive, none of us said a word.

There was an eerie silence—the kind of silence that fills a space when no one has the emotional capacity to speak. We just sat with our grief. Each of us lost in our own thoughts.

The flight on the airplane was no different. No one was talking. No one knew what to say, and no one had the energy to try. What I would have given to know what my mother was feeling—how she was processing the loss of her only son to suicide.

This would be the second child she would have to bury.

I kept thinking about how terrible that must feel. I wondered if losing Rodger would change something in her. Would she begin to see her remaining children differently? Would she stop taking us for granted?

These thoughts spun around and around in my head. I sat there in silence, quietly sobbing, unable to speak.

I could barely stand listening to the other passengers laughing and talking about their vacation plans. Their joy felt like a foreign language I couldn't translate.

A flight attendant noticed my tears, but she never stopped to ask if we needed anything. I assumed she didn't know what to say and was afraid of saying the wrong thing. So instead, she said nothing at all. She simply ignored us for the entire flight.

When we arrived at the terminal in Lexington, my grandparents were already there waiting. I hadn't seen them in about four years. For a brief moment, there was a flicker of warmth when they greeted us.

Then my grandmother broke out in loud sobs, right there in the terminal.

After she managed to compose herself, we walked to the car, climbed in, and drove straight to my father's house to begin the funeral arrangements.

No one was home when we got there, so we continued on to the funeral home. When we entered, my father and his wife were speaking with the funeral director. My father looked like someone I had never seen before. He actually looked sad.

There were tears in his eyes.

And despite all the years and all the pain, he was genuinely glad to see us—even my mother, his first wife.

My parents were civil to one another for approximately an hour—until my father found out that my mother was broke and would not be able to contribute toward my brother's funeral. That's when he began to unravel.

"She must be lying," he snapped. "Your mother is never out of money. What is she trying to pull this time?"

This was a typical argument between my mother and father. Neither of them ever believed a word the other said.

As I sat there listening, I felt embarrassed. Ashamed. But their disrespectful bickering was all too familiar to me.

Jack calmly explained to my father that, yes, my mother was low on funds—we had to finance her trip to Kentucky ourselves. My father's mouth dropped open. Suddenly, he realized he was going to have to pay for something that didn't directly benefit him.

I thought to myself, *If only my parents hadn't been so self-ish and self-centered... if they had invested in Rodger's well-be-ing... maybe we'd be gathering today for a wedding or gradua-tion—not a funeral.*

And if they had offered him a good upbringing—or a college education like the ones they'd received from their own parents—maybe this would have turned out differently. But their selfish choices had brought us all here. To this day. To this grief. To my brother's funeral.

My mother and father even haggled over the price of the funeral. Eventually, they asked me to pick out Rodger's casket because neither of them was emotionally capable of doing it.

What a horrible experience.

I wept throughout the entire ordeal, but somehow I managed to choose a fairly nice casket. Afterward, I had to go outside. I felt sick. My head was spinning—from my parents' nonsense, from my own grief, from everything.

Neither of them asked how I was feeling. Not once.

Maybe it was because they didn't know how. Both of them were only children. They never had the gift—or the pain—of loving a sibling.

It was a cold, wet, gray day in Versailles, Kentucky. The weather reflected exactly how I felt inside.

I stood under a big oak tree, sobbing quietly. I tried to keep it together—for my mother's sake—because I thought maybe, just maybe, she was feeling remorseful now. Maybe she finally understood how deeply she had hurt us. I couldn't imagine what it felt like to bury a second child.

My mother and her second husband had a child together in 1975. Her name was Kellie.

My mother had often said that she wished she could marry a man who loved children, so she could be a better mother. When she married Brian, she told me she had finally gotten her wish. Brian loved children, and not long after they married, Kellie was born.

I never had the privilege of knowing this child—my half-sister—because my mother kicked me out of the house before Kellie was born. I did meet her briefly on two occasions, but both times, my mother had left her with my younger sister, Ruth, to babysit.

Meanwhile, my mother and Brian would go to a local restaurant to have coffee together—something they did every night.

My mother said she did it because she needed time and space away from us kids, to unwind after a long, grueling day working as a toy sales clerk. She said we were too demanding of her time.

She had once been a schoolteacher while married to my father, but after their divorce, she refused to return to teaching. She said it was too difficult to work in the school system.

In reality, I believe she just didn't want to teach anyone anything.

Teaching demanded too much. And my mother, I think, didn't have the interpersonal resources to manage that role.

So she chose something less demanding. A toy store sales clerk.

It was just easier.

Working as a sales clerk paid significantly less, but my mother didn't seem too concerned. She received a sizeable amount of money each month from a trust fund, so income wasn't something she had to worry about.

My half-sister, Kellie, died in September 1976 at the age of one. She drowned in my mother's backyard pool.

At the time of the accident, my mother was home alone with Kellie. She later explained that she had been on the phone, busy planning a party. She claimed that Kellie must have managed to squeeze her little body through a thirty-pound sliding glass door that led to the pool, walked down the steps, and drowned—because, according to her, she never heard a thing.

We will never know the truth.

After the funeral, members of Brian's family quietly pulled me aside. They told me they didn't believe my mother had been entirely truthful about what happened. But once the burial was over, they never brought it up again.

The tragedy of Kellie's death was what brought me back into the family.

I was nineteen at the time. I had vowed, after being forcefully removed from my home at seventeen, that I would never speak to my parents again. But Kellie's death softened me.

I genuinely felt sorry for my mother.

Kellie's passing was tragic and deeply sad—but in my heart, it didn't compare to the emotional trauma I experienced when Rodger died.

Rodger and I had history, even if it was bittersweet.

As I stood outside under the oak tree, trying to hold myself together, I kept thinking that maybe—after losing two children—my mother would begin to see us differently. That she might stop taking her children for granted. That she might finally open herself to love.

But that thought, much to my amazement, turned out to be just that—a thought.

The experience of losing two children did nothing to change her.

It became painfully clear to me that my mother lacked true feelings of love or concern for anyone but herself.

The day of the first viewing service was a day of atonement for me.

Rodger was employed at the county jail as a detention deputy prior to his death. Throughout the service, Rodger's friends and coworkers came over to me and told me how much they liked him and what an unusually uplifting person he was. They spoke with warmth, with admiration, and with real affection.

The nurses he had worked with at Good Samaritan in Lexington told me how proud he was that I had become a nurse. I was stunned, and I thanked all of them for sharing this with me.

However, listening to these stories hurt me, because I had no idea he even spoke about me. I knew he had been angry with me for several years after I left Kentucky. The last time I saw Rodger was a hard day for me. I left Kentucky without much notice, and Rodger didn't understand. He was so angry. He just sat on the floor while the movers loaded the van. That was the last time I actually saw him. That moment stayed with me, and remembering it broke my heart.

Leaving Kentucky was the only thing I could do to save my son, Joshua, from the family's alcoholism. In the three months I had lived in Kentucky after graduating from nursing school in North Carolina, neither my brother nor my father were sober much of the time. They said and did things that were inappropriate and mean-spirited.

In order to avoid repeating the cycle of alcoholism that ran through our family, my survival instincts kicked in, and I ran. In college, I learned about the patterns that addiction follows. I was frightened for my child, and with good reason.

I knew when I left that Rodger was drinking too much. But my responsibility was to my child. At the time of Rodger's death, I had not seen him for four years. We spoke very little.

I tried to notify Rodger of my wedding and invite him to the ceremony, but I was not speaking to my father, and my mother did not know Rodger's current address. The wedding invitation was returned to me with the words "address unknown." I regret not swallowing my pride and contacting my father for Rodger's address. But I was young, I was happy, and I was getting married. I was unaware of how final life's events can be.

At that joyful time in my life, I thought the best thing I could do was to be a little less judgmental of my brother and wait for him to reach out when he was ready. I had heard from my parents that Rodger had been in rehabilitation for his drinking, so I believed he was working on his sobriety and would contact me when he could.

The next time I saw Rodger, he was lying in a coffin.

Seeing him lying there, motionless, caused a flood of guilt to rise inside me. I had left him when I knew he needed me. It was too much for me to handle. Suddenly, I could not catch my breath, and I ran outside. My husband followed me and, in his panic, he smacked my face, thinking it might help me "snap out of it." It took me a little while to calm down, but eventually, I was able to return to the viewing and appear to be in control.

The next day was the funeral service. It was just as difficult to get through.

When it was time for the funeral procession, we followed it to one of the oldest cemeteries—Lexington Cemetery—where many Confederate soldiers are buried and where my mother has a family plot. Rodger loved that cemetery, and it felt right for him to be buried there.

As we drove through the city, I could see cars stopping to allow us to go by. I thought about how utterly devastating this all was.

As a nurse, I began to reflect. I remembered how, while working in the emergency room, I had once made fun of people who came in after attending a funeral. They would be experiencing full-blown anxiety attacks and acting out in ways that, at the time, seemed over the top.

I thought they were faking it. I believed they were just seeking attention.

Now, I realized how unempathetic I had been.

Sitting in the limousine, directly behind my brother's hearse, I watched as people pulled over and stood still while we passed. I wondered if they were curious about who had died or if they even cared.

And in that moment, I understood how much deeper my compassion had become.

My brother was a Veteran, so his casket was draped with the American flag. As we drove through town, I sat motionless and watched as the flag slowly slipped off the casket. I cried. But I also felt proud of his military accomplishments.

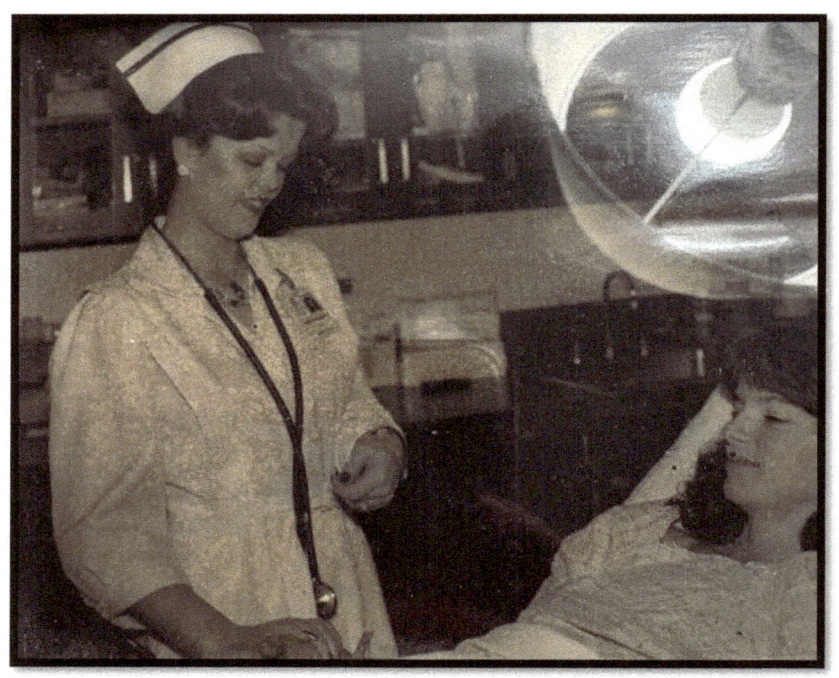

When we reached the cemetery gate, I saw our family name listed on the burial roster: Burial at 11:00 AM, Rodger Dunavent, November 8, 1988.

During the burial service, a large gust of wind blew down the wreath that our family had sent. It read, "To our dear departed brother and son."

Later that evening, my mother said the gust of wind was Rodger's way of letting us know he was with us, but that he was confused. I just shook my head. I had learned not to argue with the things my mother would say.

After Rodger was buried, we all decided to go to dinner at a local restaurant that had been one of his favorites. The name of the restaurant was Rogers.

So, in Rodger's honor, we went to eat at Rogers. But, being an alcoholic family, the real reason we went was to get drunk.

I got smashed.

It helped numb the pain for a while.

Oddly enough, we all seemed to have a pretty good time, sitting around the table, talking about Rodger and how much we missed him.

But through the viewing, the service, the burial, and later at my father's home, something felt off. My mother was more alive, more talkative, and far more jubilant than I thought was appropriate.

All she could talk about that evening was her involvement in the occult. I hadn't known she was involved in anything like that.

After the funeral, all of us—my mother, her husband, and the rest of the family—stayed at my father's house in Versailles.

It felt absurd to me that my mother would choose to stay there instead of getting a hotel room.

After we arrived, my mother began telling my sister Ruth and me that she felt Rodger's presence in the room.

She asked us if we could feel a coldness in the air. She said that if we could, it meant Rodger was stepping through us to let us know he was okay, but confused. She said he could see us, but didn't understand why he couldn't communicate.

Then she asked if we noticed the object on my father's mantle swaying above the chimney flue.

She said the movement meant Rodger was walking around in the room.

Mother told us to sit quietly, and she would speak to him because she was a medium. She said she had the knowledge, the power, and the connection to the afterlife. Mother stated that she had to do all this before midnight, because only the true white occult could summon good spirits to communicate with the living. After midnight, she said, the bad demons could enter your domain.

My mother told us to speak to Rodger and inform him that he was dead, and that he needed to move toward the light. But before leaving us, if he was troubled about his death, she asked that he communicate with us by giving some sort of a message.

Mother then spoke directly to Rodger and said, if you were murdered, knock on the wall one time. If you took your own life, knock twice.

Then there was a big bang on the wall.

Followed by a second bang.

Mother said, "Hear that? Rodger is telling us he was murdered."

I never fully believed that moment. But there were, undeniably, one or two bangs.

Up until this point, suicide was the only explanation anyone had spoken aloud. Now, my mother was introducing the idea that Rodger may have been murdered.

I immediately turned to her and asked what in the world she was talking about. She said it made perfect sense.

According to both the coroner and Rodger's girlfriend, Charla, he had been depressed.

But my mother began to question that. She asked, how do we know he was really depressed? As far as she was concerned, she had just spoken to Rodger a few days before his death. He had told her everything was fine. He mentioned that he had recently received a raise, and that he was planning to go to Alabama to reconcile with the woman he truly loved, Shawna.

So why, my mother asked, would he kill himself now?

She believed it must have been a love triangle. Charla, she assumed, had been jealous of Rodger's plans to go to Alabama. My mother became convinced that Charla was the one who shot and killed him.

There was no way to prove that Charla had done anything. Especially not with the official coroner's report ruling Rodger's death a suicide.

Still, my mother immediately called for Brian, her husband, who was a police officer, and asked him to join the conversation. She asked Brian if he would call the coroner the next day and inquire about the possibility of Rodger's death being a homicide.

Brian agreed to her request. He also mentioned that he didn't fully agree with the coroner's report either.

During this conversation, I realized something. I believed my parents were grasping for an answer that didn't reflect badly on them as parents. Maybe this was how they were coping. Suicide carries a certain shame. A sense of failure. A heaviness that can be unbearable.

Still, it was good that we were talking about it as a family. These things should be discussed.

For a moment, I allowed myself to believe that maybe this tragedy would finally wake my parents up. That it might open their hearts. That it might lead to healing.

This was an opportunity to face the reality that the family dynamics may have played a significant part in my brother's depression and his inability to cope.

But the coroner refused to reopen the case and stood by the original ruling. Cause of death: suicide.

My mother was furious.

The day after the funeral was unlike any day I would wish on anyone.

The landlord of Rodger's apartment called my father and informed him that Rodger's belongings needed to be cleared out by 5:00 p.m. that same day. My father asked all of us to go with him. He said he just couldn't do it alone.

So Jack, my mother, my stepfather, and I went to Rodger's apartment.

When we arrived, there was the yellow police tape still covering the door. I did not want to go in there because I was scared of what I might see. As my father opened the door, we took a deep breath, expecting to see a real mess, but there were no obvious signs that a thirty-year-old man had shot himself just four days earlier with his own 38-revolver.

The apartment was neat and clean, and there was candy still left over from Halloween. Rodger's cigarettes were lying on the coffee table like he had just stepped out and would return shortly. So far, I was coping, but my heart was breaking.

As we were packing his things, I noticed a record on the turntable that I hadn't seen in years; it was *The Moody Blues, Seventh Sojourn*. Seeing this album broke me into some heavy crying. I slid the record into the jacket cover and prepared to take it home with me. My father said, "Take whatever you want."

I began to pack his clothing. I could smell the faint aroma of his cologne on the shirt hanging in his closet. I fell to my knees and yelled out to the family, "I cannot continue to do this because it is such an invasion of my brother's privacy." I said, "This is making me sick to my stomach." I had to go outside and get some air.

I eventually picked out a few things that I wanted to take with me in remembrance of my brother, so I chose his stethoscope and his antique medicine cabinet. These two items had significant meaning to me.

Prior to Rodger's occupation as a detention deputy, he was employed as an orderly. His first position as an orderly was because of my recommendation to the Director of Nursing at Caldwell Memorial Hospital in North Carolina.

Rodger was a good orderly. Everyone enjoyed working with him, and I was equally pleased to have my brother work with me. One day, the Director of Nursing thanked me for bringing him to Caldwell Memorial. I felt really proud of him.

Rodger entered the nursing profession through me; he loved it and was so good at it. This is why I chose the stethoscope and the antique medicine cabinet. My father took his furniture, and my mother took his picture of Jesus Christ. My parents gave his car to Charla.

Dismantling a loved one's home is a terrible thing to have to do. The whole process involves a tedious and heart-wrenching dilemma of being tortured to see and touch things that you knew were very private. The essence

of his life was everywhere, and my heart was eternally broken.

The next day, I left Kentucky to fly back home, and as
I sat silently in the seat on the airplane, I thought that in
just four days, I had learned of my brother's death, I had
flown to Kentucky, picked out a casket, endured a heart-
wrenching ceremony, buried my little brother, and dis-
mantled his world. I was flying home a different person,
and I was frightened at how I was going to handle my
grief.

CHAPTER 2

FALLING APART QUIETLY

The next day we flew back to Florida. I was still in shock, and I did not want to talk to anyone. I just sat in the seat on the plane, silently weeping and feeling so sick to my stomach. The sadness sat so heavy in my chest that even breathing felt like effort. I knew that I had to keep it together for my child and for my new family. The death of my brother, by his own hand, was such a tragedy, and the grief was unbearable.

I went back to work the following week as a dialysis nurse. I thought that returning to work right away would help me cope. I believed that structure would hold me together.

My schedule at the dialysis center was three days a week for fourteen hours, but the work was labor intensive. As each day went by, I felt proud of myself for returning to work so soon after a tragedy and proud that I was trying to do the right thing for my family.

However, my husband was not pleased with the amount of money I was earning. He would ridicule and humiliate me. He would yell at me to work more hours and earn more income. When I tried to explain to Jack that I was doing the best I could, considering what I had just gone through, Jack only got angrier. He told me to get over it and move on. Then Jack said something so cruel that I could hardly believe a husband could say it.

Jack said, "Rodger meant nothing to me. I did not even know him. Now I have to suffer this nonsense over some-one who is dead and meant nothing to me."

This was the beginning of my decline into a hell that I was not prepared for, and the beginning of the end of the feelings I once had for Jack. I had no idea that my decline into depression would cost me so many years of my life and my marriage. But once it started, I could not stop the progression.

I began having trouble sleeping at night. I would sit up until four in the morning, unable to rest. When I finally did fall asleep, it was only to sleep the entire day away. Often, I would call out of work because I could not manage working, even if it was only three days a week. My hygiene began to slip. Sometimes I would not bathe for several days. Just existing took so much effort.

Jack never looked past his own frustration. He felt cheated out of the version of me he thought he had married. He refused to feel any empathy for what I was going through. He could not or would not see that I was literally dying right beside him, and he was not going to do anything to help me.

Now, in my desperation of not being able to live up to my husband's pressure to earn more money, and coupled with my own wish to escape this nightmare of failing my family, and my grief about Rodger, I swallowed a bottle of Percodan along with a bottle of Jack Daniels. My mind was in a dark place, and this combination felt like the only way out of the pain I was drowning in. Several hours later, I was vomiting uncontrollably in the bathroom, and Jack heard all the commotion and came in to see what was going on. He yelled very loudly, "What have you gone and done? What is the matter with you? Are you crazy?"

I had taken the overdose of pills slowly over two hours starting at around 10:00 p.m. earlier that night. Each pill, each sip, felt like a desperate attempt to quiet the storm inside me. Jack became very angry. He called my mother and told her that he just did not know what to do with me anymore and that he was going to bring me to Port St. Lucie and she could figure out what to do with me.

My mother did not have a chance to tell Jack no. We arrived at my mother's around 10:00 A.M. the following morning. Jack dropped me and then drove back to Ft. Lauderdale. Jack said he had to get back to his business.

Not even my current emotional crisis was important enough for Jack to miss a day at his plant. Jack and his father owned a wholesale seafood distributing company.

All the items were perishable in just a few days. Jack's father would frequently take off time to help his wife with her illness, but Jack would not help me.

When Jack dumped me at my mother's house, I felt even more unwanted and not worth the trouble or the time, and I was becoming quite ill. Jack's father and one of his co-workers, named Steve, were telling Jack that I was just a liability and to get rid of me before I became too costly.

I knew that Jack's family felt this way about me because Jack told me. And prior to my marriage to Jack, Steve had informed me that Jack often spoke badly about my child at work and in front of Steve and Jack's father, Jack Sr. Steve said that Jack told everyone at work that he could hardly stand to be around my son, Joshua. Steve thought that I ought to know this. I told Steve I appreciated the information. Learning about this made me so upset and unhappy.

That night, I talked with Jack about what Steve had told me, and Jack reassured me that that was not the case at all. Jack stated that, in fact, he looked forward to his relationship with Joshua as his stepfather. I believed this because I wanted it to be true, but I would find out the truth down the road. In fact, Jack would tell me years later that he really envied Joshua because my son had everything going for him in the areas of physical size and scholastic aptitude that Jack never possessed.

After Jack left me at my mother's, all I did was stare into space. I was despondent. My mother realized that I was in trouble, and she did not want to be stuck taking care of me, so she made an appointment with a local psychiatrist, Dr. E. Balo in Port St. Lucie. Treatment with this doctor was my first step towards emotional health.

When I arrived at Dr. Balo's office, I was almost catatonic. I could not find the ability to speak. My mother had to speak for me. Then the doctor asked me to come into her office without my mother, and she said softly, "Laura, how can I help you if you do not tell me what is wrong?" I burst into tears, crying so uncontrollably. Again, I could not speak. However, I was able to manage to inform the doctor that I was really not sure what was the matter with me. She asked me why I took the pills. I told her I took them because I could no longer live with this agony. She encouraged me to admit myself voluntarily to the psychiatric hospital so she could have nurses, therapists, and herself look after me for a while during this period where my life was really meaningless to me. Along with the suicide gesture, she felt placing me in a hospital under a suicide watch would be appropriate until I felt better. I agreed.

CHAPTER 3

THE BREAKDOWN BEGINS

I was admitted to a private psychiatric hospital in Ft. Pierce, Florida. The doctor recommended a thirty-day in-patient treatment plan. When I arrived, I felt too sick to care.

I did smoke cigarettes. Because I wanted to smoke, I had to come out of my room and go into the general population room and sit among the other patients while I had my cigarette. Having to leave my room in order to smoke forced me to interact with the other inmates, or "crazies," and I was in no mood for that.

One man started walking over to me and began a conversation about nonsense. I was annoyed, but he seemed friendly. He introduced himself as Tim. He mentioned that he had met another woman in the hospital named Jeannie and that he thought I might like to talk with her, since she was around my age.

So he introduced us.

We spoke for a little while, and then I went off to bed. I was exhausted.

In the morning, Tim re-introduced me to Jeannie. She did appear to be friendly and receptive to Tim's suggestion that the three of us hang out together. He said we seemed to be "the least crazy of the whole group."

I laughed.

The tension one feels when admitted to a psychiatric hospital is disturbing enough, and that's before adding the crushing emotional pain that even qualifies you for admission.

Meeting Tim and Jeannie turned out to be beneficial in my immediate healing phase. They gave me a sense of camaraderie, and someone to talk to who was also experiencing the same feelings of hopelessness and the desire to die.

The three of us listened to each other's stories as best we could.

But I tended to stay on a superficial level.

I didn't really know how to explain what was wrong, or why I had ended up here. I had no real understanding of what was happening inside me—no clue as to why I was in this predicament of being clinically depressed.

But I was about to learn.

The therapist had requested that I meet with her the next morning to discuss my admission. All night, I dreaded this meeting. I did not want to talk to anyone. I just wanted to sleep, smoke cigarettes, cry, be left alone, and virtually just turn into a slug. I didn't want to be analyzed, questioned, or prodded. I only wanted silence.

The therapist's name was Joan. She called for me, just as she said she would, at 9:00 A.M.

When I arrived in her office, she looked easy enough to get along with. She was older, about fifty years of age. She had a friendly and welcoming persona. There was a calmness about her, a maternal warmth that didn't feel forced. She asked me to please sit down and make myself as comfortable as possible so I could best enjoy our session together.

I sat down feeling uptight and uncomfortable, hating every moment of having survived my suicide attempt and having to subject myself to this torture. My skin felt tight. My body sat tense, like I was bracing for impact.

Joan started off our session with the question, "So, Laura, tell me why you voluntarily admitted yourself to our facility?"

I told her that Dr. Balo felt I needed time away from my surroundings and the stresses that were causing me great discomfort. Dr. Balo felt that I needed supervision of my life right now because of my suicide attempt.

Joan asked me to try and tell her what stresses I thought were causing me such discomfort that I would try to harm myself.

I began with the fact that my husband was putting pressure on me to work more hours and earn more money as a nurse, like I had been doing prior to my brother's death. But I could no longer work the way I had been. I was dealing with my grief alone. I had no support systems to help me cope with my day-to-day anguish. No one to help ease the pressure of pretending everything was fine, of keeping up appearances, of smiling for my child while breaking inside.

I told her that every day I woke up was like dragging my body through concrete. That I wasn't just tired—I was completely depleted.

Joan smiled and said, "Wow. How insightful, and how wonderful it is to have you as a client because you are able to tell me exactly what it is that is troubling you in a concise and understandable manner."

Joan went on to say that even though she didn't yet know the full extent of my depression or my story, she was excited because she believed she could help me.

Joan asked me to tell her more about myself.

I told her that I was thirty-three years old and that I had married a year ago, for the second time. I told her I had one child from my first marriage, and his name was Joshua, and that he was going to be ten years old in a few days.

I went on to tell Joan how very proud I was of Joshua and what a wonderful child he was. I proceeded to tell her how well he did in school and how popular he was. He had this kindness in him, a light that drew people in. Joshua was able to get along with anybody—unlike me growing up—because I had instilled in him a sense of confidence, and he knew he was loved.

I told her I had made it my mission to give him everything I never had. And I meant every word.

Having been raised by unloving parents, I knew that to be loved and cared for by a parent was everything. By being a loving and caring parent, it creates a foundation for children to thrive and live up to their potential. I felt proud of myself for having been a parent who created an environment for my child to be able to grow up in a safe and happy place, so he could have a chance at being a well-adjusted and happy adult. It was one of the only things in my life I felt sure I had done right.

Joan asked me, if I were to take my life, how would that affect Joshua and his survival? This was a powerful and awakening statement.

Up until Joan's question, I truly thought that Joshua would be better off without me around in this condition. I believed that in the event of my death, my son would have a substantial sum of life insurance money to go on in life without my emotional baggage. This I truly believed. It seemed like the more practical option. It felt like I was saving him from me.

I felt like I was going to undo all the teachings I had given him in the past because I felt so unglued, so insecure, and completely crazy. I did not have the energy anymore to be a good parent. All I wanted to do was disappear, with my son remembering me the way I had been, instead of the broken version of who I had become.

I had been depressed most of my life.

The way Joan asked me how I thought Joshua would do in the event of my death—it carried a tone that struck me. In her voice, I sensed that she believed he would not do too well without me. I stated this observation to her, and she agreed with my interpretation.

Joan went on to educate me about the statistics concerning the children of parent(s) who commit suicide. I was told that a large number of these children tend to replicate their parents and die by suicide.

The statistics that children who have had a parent die by suicide are at a far greater risk of taking their own lives later in life dumbfounded me. I felt like vomiting.

I had not known this. I was very upset hearing these statistics. I have always been big on knowing statistics, and I felt stupid that I had never come across this, or if I had, I had forgotten. Suddenly, I wasn't just scared for myself. I was scared for my child.

All I ever wanted for my child was for him to never have to experience life anywhere similar to my experiences. I wanted him to be happy and to see the glass as half full.

Joshua was brought up to believe that he was the beginning of a healthy family pattern. I always told him this. Sometimes, I felt Joshua might think he was burdened by that statement, but I believed it was the truth, and it gave both of us hope for the future.

I had hope for him.

I did not want to take away the only gift I could give him—which was a chance to be a healthier person—by committing a selfish act of *suicide*.

CHAPTER 4

KENTUCKY, MY CAGE

Joan had me thinking. Once again, my survival instincts were kicking in. Getting better—getting out of this hospital—that was all I could focus on. But Joan wasn't here just to check in on my vitals. She wanted to go deeper. She gently started to dig, asking me to talk about my childhood.

I took a deep breath and a long pause. Then I decided: I'd try. I'd give it my best shot.

"Start with your earliest memory," she said softly.

The first real memory I have—one that still burns vividly in my mind—is from when I was five. We were living in Lexington, Kentucky, in a subdivision called Lansdowne Estates. Our house was on Bramer Drive. My mother stayed home with Rodger and me, while my father was out at work.

This memory is etched into me, probably because of how traumatic it was.

As usual, I was left to entertain myself. I had found my sparkler paints in a closet upstairs and started playing. I don't remember what I was painting—probably just smearing color on paper—but I do remember the mess. Paint everywhere. I was lost in it, until my mother found me.

She lost it.

Screaming. Raging. Her face contorted with anger, her voice sharp and terrifying. I had opened the paints without her permission. That alone was enough to unleash a storm.

"You're really going to get it when your father comes home," she snapped, dragging me to my room and slamming the door.

And so I waited. Five hours. Alone in that room, every minute stretching like it would never end. For a five-year-old, it was eternity. I prayed that my father would take pity on me. That he'd be kind. But he wasn't.

When he got home, she wasted no time. "You need to punish her," she told him coldly. And he obeyed.

My parents didn't just discipline us—they relished the power they had. They created a world ruled by fear. My father called me down to his bedroom. He told me to remove my underpants, lean over his bed, and hold perfectly still. "If you move," he warned, "you'll get more licks."

Of course I moved. I was five. My hands kept trying to protect myself. I begged him not to hit me.

"Please, Daddy… please don't…"

My pleading only made him angrier. He took off his belt.

I held my breath. Time froze. The moment before the first hit felt endless. I moved again. That was enough for him to lose all control. He picked me up, placed me across his knees, and began to whip me with the belt.

At one point, I slammed my forehead against the foot-board of the bed. I was dazed. Everything went blurry.

That's when he stopped.

My mother had been standing in the doorway the entire time, watching. For once, her expression changed. She looked afraid.

They thought they had gone too far.

Both of my parents worked in child welfare. They knew exactly what a head injury could mean—especially if someone else found out. My mother quickly ran to get ice. My father left the room without a word, detached from the whole thing, and went to watch TV.

Joan noticed the tears in my eyes. She told me we could stop. But I shook my head, took another breath, and went on.

The bump on my forehead swelled to the size of a golf ball. Part of me wished it had been worse. Maybe then someone would've stepped in. Maybe then the beatings would've stopped. But nothing changed. The incident was never mentioned again.

Still, it left its scar.

There were more beatings after that. Many more. A belt across the back. Yelling. Threats. Silence. I lived in fear. Home was not a safe place, so I learned to survive in my own way.

I started acting out. I hit younger kids in the neighborhood. I tormented my little brother. I started to lie, to steal—little rebellions that made me feel, briefly, like I had some control.

Somewhere in those early years, my grandmother Ruth—whom we called Maw—came to live with us for a while. I didn't understand why at the time. Only later did I learn the truth: my grandfather Johnny, nicknamed Baggy, was living on the streets of Lexington, in an area called the Bowery. He had once been an engineer, but alcohol had destroyed everything—his career, his family, his dignity.

While he spiraled, Maw found refuge with us. She didn't have a job, and she didn't say much—but she was kind to me. Kinder than anyone else in that house. I looked forward to being around her.

But my mother didn't like that.

When she noticed how close I was becoming to Maw, she made it clear: no affection. No hugs. No warmth. If I wanted my mother's acceptance, I had to reject my grandmother.

It was the first time I remember love being punished.

So I chose my mother. I buried the affection I felt for my grandmother deep inside me. But sometimes, I slipped. And when I did, my mother would say things like,

"Stay away from your grandmother. She's no good. She's crazy. She doesn't love anybody."

Even as my mother said those cruel things, I still risked being near my grandmother. Because even in her most eccentric moments, she never treated me the way my mother did.

My mother made me choose—her or my grandmother. And I knew what that choice meant. If I didn't stay away from my grandmother, I'd lose whatever scraps of attention and affection my mother gave me. That was the price. It was survival, and I paid it in silence. But the sadness of that decision never really left me. I chose my mother, but I still found ways to sneak time with my grandmother, to feel the safety she gave me, even if it was brief.

One summer afternoon, I was visiting my grandmother. She told me I could play in the fort behind our garage—a dusty old space that felt like a secret world. Inside, I found a rack of beautiful formal gowns hanging just inside the door. They weren't covered or protected from the musty air, but to me they looked magical.

Later that day, I invited some friends over and showed them the dresses. We played dress-up and twirled around, planning to surprise my grandmother and show off our look. It was innocent fun.

Then my mother arrived.

The second she saw us in those gowns, she exploded. I didn't know the dresses were hers. In front of all my friends, she screamed at me, ripped the dress off my body, and demanded that the others remove theirs immediately. Her rage was blistering. "Get in the car right now," she yelled. My friends were told to leave. No explanation. Just fury.

I was mortified. Humiliated beyond words. But underneath that, I was afraid—terrified of what would come next.

Her outburst made it feel like I had burned down the house. Her voice echoed in my ears, full of hatred and disgust. And of course, like always, she told me to go to my room and wait for my father to come home. I knew what that meant. Another beating. My friends ran home, shaken and afraid.

By now, I had started to hate and fear my mother. Her anger was unpredictable. When anything upset her—anything at all—she unleashed it on me. For a long time, I thought something was wrong with me. I blamed myself for why kids didn't want to play with me. So did my parents. But looking back, I realize now—it wasn't me. It was them. Our family was the one people avoided.

The neighbors knew. I'm sure they warned their children to stay away from our house—the house with the unstable mother, the alcoholic father who was often absent, the drunk grandfather, and the "crazy" grandmother. People saw more than I realized back then.

I told Joan about my father, too. The earliest memory I have of him is from when I was seven. What I remember most isn't an event—it's a feeling. A creepy, uneasy feeling whenever I was alone with him. I avoided being alone with him as much as I could. I never understood why, and

I still don't have a clear explanation.

But Joan helped me see it differently.

She told me that children who experience early trauma often block out the specific memories. Just because I couldn't remember the details didn't mean the fear was imaginary. In fact, she said it likely meant something did happen—something I couldn't yet face. That was the first time I began to understand that I had been a victim. Not just of anger or beatings, but of real parental abuse.

Whenever I tried to talk to someone in my family— my parents, my siblings—about anything that had happened, they shut me down. "Drop it." "Move on." "Stop living in the past." If I remembered something they didn't like, they would twist the story and tell me, "That's not how it happened."

They worked hard to erase my memories.

Sometimes they went even further. They told me I made it all up. I'd try to talk about something that had scarred me, and they'd say, "What's wrong with you?

When are you going to stop blaming your parents and take responsibility for your own life?"

But I wasn't trying to blame them. I was just trying to make sense of it. I was desperate for clarity. I needed help.

As I got older, stepping into adulthood, the confusion only grew. I began to see how deeply those years had wounded me. I started realizing that I needed answers. I would have forgiven them—both of them—if only they had explained why they were the way they were. If only they had told us, even once, that they were struggling.

Why couldn't they just say, "We were going through something hard"?

If they had confided in us as children, I believe I would've understood. I would've had compassion. But instead, they built walls, hid behind anger, and left us—left me—alone with the madness.

Joan made me feel safe. And that safety allowed me to finally open up and speak about the things I had been carrying alone for so long. The things no child should ever have to hold. She helped me begin to unravel the confusion I had lived with, especially the fear I felt around my father. As a child, I could never understand why I never wanted to be alone with him. I only knew that something about it felt wrong.

That feeling stayed with me, and it made my life difficult in ways I could not explain. One day, I came home from school with straight A's. I should have been happy. But that day took a turn when my mother insisted that my father take me out for dinner to celebrate. Just the two of us.

The thought alone made my stomach turn. I hoped he would refuse, using the excuse that it was a school night. But he didn't. My mother kept pushing him to show some interest in my achievements, and eventually he gave in.

He drove me to dinner in Lexington, to a part of town called Chevy Chase near the University of Kentucky. I managed to get through the car ride without panicking. My father barely spoke, and I was grateful for the silence.

When we entered the restaurant, a woman with a large beehive hairdo greeted us almost immediately and led us to a table. She seemed to recognize him. Throughout the meal, even at seven years old, I could tell there was something strange about the way she acted. She was overly attentive, laughing too loudly, smiling too much. I didn't have the vocabulary at the time, but I knew she was flirting with my father. Her attention made me uncomfortable.

After we finished eating, my father told me to go wait in the car while he paid the bill. I sat outside, alone, without the heat on, growing colder by the minute. Time passed. He still hadn't come out.

Eventually, I got up the courage to go back inside and look for him. As I approached, I saw him; my father and the waitress in the alcove. They were kissing.

The moment he saw me, his face darkened. He snapped at me to go back to the car. The ride home was completely silent. You could hear the tires on the road, but not a word between us.

Then he broke the silence. He told me not to tell my mother. He said it wasn't what it looked like. He explained that the woman was an old friend who had always been in love with him, and he didn't want to hurt her feelings. He told me my mother would not understand. I didn't respond. I just nodded, agreeing not to say anything.

I never told. But I never forgot.

I didn't know why that memory stayed with me so vividly. Later in life, I would learn the truth. Her name was Carol Bond. She wasn't just some old friend. She was the woman my father had a long, secret affair with, one that would last over twenty years. And she would reappear in my life when I was a teenager, in ways that were deeply damaging.

That night was only the beginning. It was the first clear sign of how little regard my father had for me, for our family, for our safety. His selfishness would continue to surface in ways that hurt all of us. He exposed us to people and situations that put us in harm's way. Some of it was physical, much of it emotional. None of it was forgettable.

Even though I stayed silent about what I saw, my mother already knew. Her instincts had been screaming at her for a long time.

One night, when my father didn't come home, my mother erupted. She raged at me and Rodger, screaming about what a lowlife, cheating man he was. I cried, begging her to stop, insisting that she was wrong. I told her I didn't believe it.

She called me stupid. She said I was blind and pathetic for defending him. Her words stung deeply, and her anger terrified us. Rodger and I were in tears. We were just children. It hurt to hear your mother talk about your father like that, even when you suspected she might be right.

In her fury, she suddenly ordered us into the car. It was nine at night. We were in our pajamas, and it was a school night. But none of that mattered. She said we were going out for ice cream.

We drove into Lexington, right back to the area she knew my father liked. She bought us ice cream, then drove up and down the streets of Chevy Chase, ranting about how she would catch him in the act. We never found him that night. But when he came home later, their fight was unbearable.

They screamed, slammed doors, cursed. They didn't care that we were there, listening. They never did. It was always about them, never about us.

A few days later, my mother told Rodger and me to get in the car again. This time she said she was going to prove, once and for all, what kind of man our father really was.

We drove to Versailles.

And she found him.

There he was. With Carol Bond. Cozy and comfortable. No guilt, no shame. As if it were all perfectly normal.

That was the day I stopped believing in the illusion of family. That was the day everything changed.

Once again, her name appeared in my life. Carol Bond. My mother had successfully proven to Rodger and me that our father was, in her words, a no-good, cheating bastard. That night planted something deep inside me, something that would affect every relationship I would ever have with men. It never really left me.

Not long after that, we were uprooted again. This time, we were headed to Orlando, Florida. It was the summer of 1963. I never understood the reason for the move, and I understood even less why we returned to Kentucky just a few months later. No one ever talked about it. It was as if it never happened.

When we did return, we moved into my father's childhood home in the small town of Midway, Kentucky. Of all the places I lived as a child, Midway felt the safest. The town was small and quiet, and my grandmother lived right behind us.

Living there meant that my parents had to behave, at least more than usual. The town had no tolerance for inappropriate behavior, and everyone knew everyone. That seemed to keep them in check. Unfortunately, our time there was short-lived. The next year, we moved again. This time to another small town in the mountains called Irvington.

Years later, my father gave me his version of why we moved to Irvington. He said he had been offered a position with the school system, and he accepted the job on the condition that they also hire my mother. My mother, on the other hand, said the move was not a career opportunity but an escape. According to her, my father had been kicked out of the Woodford and Fayette County school systems and could no longer work as a welfare counselor at Kentucky Village. She said he had been caught fraternizing with students.

My father went ahead to Irvington one week before the rest of us. He told my mother to drive us all up the following Saturday. That included our dog, Dale. The drive was terrifying. The road to Irvington was full of steep, winding mountain turns. At one point, the brakes failed completely. We were lucky not to have gone off a cliff.

We stopped at a service station, shaken. The mechanic, as my mother told it, said the brake line had been deliberately cut. My mother didn't hesitate. She looked right at Rodger and me and said she was certain our father had done it. She believed he was trying to kill us for the insurance money so he could be with his new girlfriend, Jackie.

I was horrified. I sat there silently, tears falling down my cheeks. The woman she was referring to, Jackie, was someone my father had supposedly met at a honky-tonk. According to my mother, that was the reason he moved us to this little town. To be near her.

The moment we arrived in Irvington, my mother confronted him. He denied everything, of course. He said he would never do something like that. But not long after, another wave of chaos hit. One day, I came home and found my mother visibly shaken. She told me that someone at the school where my father worked had exposed a terrible secret. According to her, the school administrator had revealed that my father was trying to hire his girlfriend's brother to murder her. Maybe all of us.

Everything happened quickly after that. Rodger and I were sent to stay with our grandparents. My parents left for the Bahamas. My grandmother told us they had to go because my father was trying to escape the fallout from the murder-for-hire plot. They were gone for a week.

When they returned, they acted like nothing had happened. Like two people who had just enjoyed a relaxing vacation. There was no conversation about the horror we had just lived through, no concern for the fear they had left behind in us. And not long after they came back, we moved again. This time, we were heading back to Midway.

By now, I felt dizzy from the constant change. I was only eight years old and had already attended five different schools. It would continue like that all through high school. I never stayed anywhere long enough to grow roots. Making friends became nearly impossible. Every time we moved, the neighbors would whisper. Everyone could see how chaotic and strange our family was.

When we returned to Midway, I felt a small flicker of joy. But it didn't last. Not long after we arrived, my dog Dale disappeared. I was devastated. I begged my mother to help me find him. She looked at me coldly and told me she had seen some vans in the area. She believed they were from a research lab and that they had stolen Dale to experiment on him.

Hearing that broke something in me. The thought of my dog being taken, tortured, used in experiments—it was unbearable. What kind of person says something like that to a child? Dale never came back. And from that moment on, I hated animal testing. I have spent my life supporting animal rescue and ethical treatment of animals. I never forgot Dale.

That same year, I entered the third grade at Midway Elementary. It was a beautiful, historic school, over a hundred years old. My father and grandparents had attended that same school. For a moment, I started to feel like I belonged somewhere.

But just as I was starting to settle in, my parents decided we were leaving again. This time, we were heading to Florida for the winter. They hated the cold, and they loved the idea of Florida.

We traveled all the way to the Keys by car. Back in the 1960s, that kind of trip was long and difficult. The interstate highway system was not yet complete, so we had to take mountain roads through Georgia to reach Florida.

As usual, my mother found ways to make the trip terrifying. Rodger and I were told to sit in the backseat for three days without making a sound. If we acted out, we were warned, we would "get it good." That meant being hit.

Most people know how hard it is for children to sit still for hours on end. When we misbehaved, my mother would turn around, climb to her knees in the front seat, and pinch our legs until we screamed. That was her way of keeping us quiet.

I remember those moments as clearly as if they happened yesterday.

I am sorry, Joan. I had to stop here. I needed to breathe. I left the room and just broke down in tears. I walked outside and smoked a cigarette. When I finally composed myself, I came back to the counseling room. Joan smiled at me. She told me I was doing an incredible job and that she understood how exhausting it was. She gently encouraged me to continue. She said this process was helping me heal.

So I picked up where I left off. I talked about the rest of the trip to Marathon, Florida. It took three long days to get there. We stayed in a botel, a boat hotel, in a place called Key Colony Beach. The place was beautiful. The ocean shimmered, and the sun seemed to make everything softer.

For all the pain and confusion in my life, I did love to swim. Being near the water gave me a rare sense of peace.

During our stay in Florida, Rodger and I were enrolled in a winter school since we would be there for two months. That meant yet another new school, another new group of kids, and another attempt at making friends. I was only eight years old, and I already felt exhausted by the emotional labor of starting over again and again.

While we were in Marathon, I had no idea what our parents did all day. Rodger and I were mostly left on our own.

One Saturday, possibly out of boredom or maybe from acting out—I still don't really know—I stole a horse pin from a gift shop I had walked to by myself. When my parents discovered the pin, they marched me back to the store, made me return it, and forced me to apologize to the owner.

My punishment for stealing was a beating with my father's fraternity paddle.

It wasn't just any paddle. It was a one-inch-thick wooden paddle, a gift from his college fraternity, complete with a handle. It was a real weapon. That paddle had already left bruises on both Rodger and me, across our backsides and even our hands.

As he prepared for the punishment, my father reminded me to stay perfectly still. If I moved, I would get extra whacks. I begged him for mercy. What was meant to be five hits turned into eight. I couldn't help but flinch.

"Joan, what's wrong?" I asked, noticing her expression.

"Laura, you remember so much of the detail. It's like you're still there, reliving it," she said quietly.

"I know, Joan. I don't understand how I can recall everything so clearly."

Joan leaned forward. "I think after the loss of your brother Rodger, your mind opened up. All of these memories came flooding in. It's likely the major reason why your depression escalated so quickly. Have you ever spoken about these incidents to anyone?"

"No," I said. "I was always told I made them up, or that they didn't happen the way I remember."

"Let's keep going," Joan said gently. "We need to get your full story before you turn fifty-five, remember?"

We both laughed a little, breaking the heaviness for a moment.

"Okay," I said, taking a deep breath. "Another incident I remember clearly from Marathon was when my parents came up with a new kind of punishment."

One day, Rodger and I decided to go fishing off the dock behind our botel. We had taken the bamboo fishing poles our parents used at night. We didn't really know what we were doing, but we were excited to try. The canal water was so clear, and it was a beautiful morning.

We set up all three poles on the dock and waited for a bite. At some point, we got hungry and went inside to make ourselves lunch. When we came back, one of the poles was gone. It had either fallen in or been pulled into the water. We couldn't see it and the water was too deep to retrieve it.

We were just six and eight years old, left alone all day near deep water, with no supervision. We had no idea where our parents were.

Later that afternoon, we told them what had happened. By normal standards, any parent would have been horrified that their young children had been left near water unsupervised. But not ours. They didn't care about our safety. They were furious that we had taken their fishing poles without permission.

They decided it was time for more punishment.

My parents always seemed to take some kind of twisted pleasure in disciplining us. Over the years, I came to realize that Rodger and I were the only people they had power over. They abused that power freely. They didn't have many friends. People tended to keep their distance. So they made us their targets.

They told us we were going to be hit ten times with the paddle for using the poles, plus an extra hit for every time we tried to shield ourselves. That day, we endured another round of pain and humiliation. I remember not being able to sit for days. Being beaten with a one-inch paddle was nothing short of sadistic.

"Kellie, I'm honestly surprised you're here today, telling me all of this," Joan said, shaking her head.

"I think Rodger died because he couldn't keep going," I replied. "He didn't want to face all of this. I know he was suffering. I had heard he started drinking heavily in his last few years."

Joan nodded. "It makes sense. We'll go over everything again when I review my notes. It's important that I understand the full picture. Please, keep going."

"By now," I said, "I had started to act out more. I was becoming a problem child."

One day, during another abusive episode, I ran from my father and cursed at him. That was enough to trigger another punishment. My father said he was going to teach me a lesson for my foul mouth. The irony was, I had learned that language from him.

He beat me fifteen times with the paddle, hard enough to leave the imprint of "Class of '56" on my skin. Then they made me lay across their laps and forced me to hold a bar of soap in my mouth until I threw up.

The lack of supervision, the cruelty—it all eventually caught up to them.

When my younger sister Ruth was three, we were all outside near the pool. Both parents were home, yet Ruth almost drowned. No one was watching. It was only by some miracle that she survived.

I had already told Joan about my half-sister Kellie, who had drowned while in my mother's care. That tragedy didn't change anything. My parents never took their responsibilities seriously. Parenting, for them, required caring about someone other than themselves, and they simply weren't capable of that.

As I spoke, I could tell Joan was disturbed. I started to weep. I had never told this story in such detail. I was listening to myself for the first time and realizing just how much I had been through. It finally made sense to me why I felt broken. Why I struggled to be liked. Why I always felt like something was wrong with me.

Joan gently suggested we take a break and continue later during the group session on women's issues and sexual abuse.

"I just want to finish what I planned to say today," I told her.

"That's fine," she said. "But I need a fifteen-minute break."

While she stepped out, I sat alone in the general room with a cigarette, reflecting on everything I had just said.

For the first time, someone had listened to me and believed me. That validation meant everything.

When we returned, I told Joan how proud I was of myself for finally speaking out. I could see she understood the depth of what I had experienced.

She said, "Laura, what you've described is traumatic enough to affect any child. I'm truly sorry that you were born to two people who didn't know how to love you."

She paused and added, "Some of what you've said mirrors parts of my own childhood. Honestly, I've been struggling to hear it, because it's bringing up things I haven't dealt with myself."

Joan was honest, and I loved her for that. I asked if she felt she could still continue as my therapist.

She looked at me and said, "Yes. I believe God brought us together. For both of us to learn, and to grow."

Through my nursing education, I had learned that many therapists are drawn to their field as part of their own healing process. When Joan opened up to me and shared some of her personal struggles, I felt a spark of something I hadn't felt in a long time. Hope. She had survived her own abusive past and was using that pain to help others. She was still growing emotionally, she said, but what she was most proud of was being a survivor. That inspired me.

Her openness gave me the strength to continue. I felt I needed to finish telling my story to move forward in my healing.

I returned to the memories from Marathon. Sadly, most of my childhood memories are clouded by abuse. The painful ones far outnumber the few moments of peace or joy.

I told Joan that during our winter stay in Marathon, my parents would often force us to stay awake in the car until the early hours of the morning while they tried to catch fish. We were expected to sleep upright in the backseat, often cold, cramped, and exhausted.

My baby sister Ruth was only a few months old at the time. She was tiny, frail, and clearly neglected. She barely made it through the trip back to Kentucky. My mother often said Ruth was born so weak because my father had forced her to take quinine tablets early in the pregnancy in an attempt to induce a miscarriage.

On the drive back to Kentucky, Ruth began having trouble breathing. We had to stop at a hospital to get her help. She was treated and released, but the memory stayed with me. My parents were so careless, so self-involved, that they continually put all of us in danger.

When we returned to Kentucky, I started fourth grade. One afternoon, I asked our housekeeper, Dottie, for permission to stay after school in Versailles to play with my friend Sandy Miller. Dottie said yes. That meant my mother would have to come pick me up. It was only a seven-mile drive, but when my mother found out, she refused. She was furious that I had stayed. Sandy's mother ended up driving me home.

When I got out of the car, I saw a tall, narrow box standing upright in the front yard. Curious, I bent the box down to look inside.

My dog Andy was in the box. He was dead.

I became hysterical. I ran to the back door and asked Dottie what had happened to my sweet poodle. She told me that one of the Denver boys had hit him with their car. She had heard the sound and rushed out to get him. In the panic, she had forgotten she had hamburgers on the stove. By the time she got back inside, the frying pan had caught fire. She tried to put it out under the sink faucet, but the curtains caught fire. The fire department had to come. The kitchen was destroyed.

My mother had been busy dealing with the insurance company and fire department all afternoon. But once she was done, she unleashed her rage on me. She screamed that it was my fault. If I had come home after school like I was supposed to, the dog would still be alive. Her kitchen would not have burned down. All of it, she said, was because of me.

Those are devastating words to tell a child. But she was my mother. I depended on her for love and protection. So I believed her.

For years, I returned to that bloodstained spot on the road, staring at it, blaming myself for Andy's death. That guilt lived in me long after the fire was put out.

As the years passed, my mother found more ways to hurt me. She would say cruel things and do even worse. I tried to be like other girls, tried to gain her approval. But every time I reached for her, she pulled away, leaving me shattered.

When I was six, I was chosen to tap dance in a performance of "The Ball and the Jack." I was proud and excited. But when I looked to my mother for praise, all she could say was how stupid I looked. I had the wrong leg pointed during the final bow. That was all she noticed.

At nine, I sang in front of the women's club in Midway. Another chance to make her proud. Instead, she told me I was the only one singing off key.

She loved to show me off in expensive dresses and send me to private school, but it always came with a price.

Christina Crawford had written about wire hangers in her memoir, and I remember reading it and feeling like she was telling my story. When I was nine, I was responsible for caring for my clothes to my mother's exact standards. If I didn't hang something correctly, she would rip it from the closet, throw it to the floor, and stomp on it. She called me ungrateful and told me I didn't deserve nice things.

She knew how much I loved one outfit in particular, a dress with an overjacket in a houndstooth print. One day, I didn't hang it to her liking. She stormed into my room and tore it to pieces in front of me. I cried until I had nothing left in me. To this day, I still love houndstooth, but I will not wear it. That memory clings to it.

When I questioned her about her cruelty later in life, she denied meaning any harm. She said I had taken her too seriously, that I had misunderstood her humor. She insisted that I had always been too sensitive, too strange. As a child, I believed everything she said. Her words were like venom, and I swallowed every drop. It would take me years to realize the damage she had done. Years to understand that I was not the problem.

Now, at thirty-three years old, I still cry for the little girl inside me. The girl who is still waiting for her mother's love. Still hoping.

Joan gently interrupted. She told me I needed to stop for the day. Her voice was soft, but her eyes were full of emotion.

She told me how sorry she was to hear all of this. She said that no child should have to endure what I had. She recommended I rest and start again in the morning.

I asked her if talking about my past was helping.

She nodded. "So many people suffer because they never get help. They carry all the weight, all the pain. What we're doing here is clearing out those old messages, the negative tapes. You're making room for healing and self-esteem."

Joan asked me to think about how I wanted to continue tomorrow. She also invited me to a support group for women who had been through physical or sexual abuse by men. I told her I would consider it.

She said she believed I needed strong support as I worked through all of this. I agreed to join the group. They were meeting the next afternoon.

I told Joan goodnight and left the counseling room. When I got back to the general room, Jeannie and Tim were there. It was almost lunchtime.

Tim looked up and asked, "How are you feeling?"

I told him I had a headache and felt completely drained.

He nodded. "Yeah, we all know how intense one-on-one sessions can be."

As the day wore on, I became increasingly agitated. The nurses gave me a medication called Sinequan to calm me down, and for the severe headache I had developed, they gave me a narcotic called Percodan. By the time both medications started working, I was no longer in control of myself.

First, I tried to escape. Then I began acting inappropriately. I remember clinging to a pole in the patio, touching it and behaving in a way that was sexual and clearly out of character. That was all it took for the nurses to label me. They decided right then that I must be manic-depressive, and they placed me in seclusion.

The next morning, Dr. Balo met with me. She asked if anyone in my family had ever been diagnosed with bipolar disorder. I told her yes—my fraternal grandmother and my cousin, Nancy Ellen, had both been institutionalized and had undergone electroconvulsive therapy. Dr. Balo said she would continue to evaluate me and encouraged me to keep working closely with my therapist so she could determine the best way to treat me. I agreed to do my part.

Joan met with me at 9:00 a.m. I continued telling my story, trying to stay chronological. That seemed to help me remember more clearly.

I picked up where I left off, back in Midway.

One afternoon, I climbed up a one-hundred-fifty-foot elevated train track. At the top, I heard a train whistle in the distance and panicked. There was still time to climb down safely, but fear took over. I slipped and slid all the way to the bottom, scraping my legs against the concrete. The pain was unbearable. The skin on my thighs was torn open. The wounds were deep, dirty, and raw.

I limped home crying, desperate for help. But instead of comfort, I was met with punishment. My father beat me for being on the tracks in the first place. Then he forced me into the bathtub, angry and disgusted that he had to deal with my injuries when he would rather have been out with one of his girlfriends.

He scrubbed my wounds so harshly that the pain was beyond description. When it was over, I collapsed from exhaustion and terror right there on the bathroom floor. I was still naked. My parents left me there.

The next morning, neither of them offered to take me to the doctor. So I took myself.

I walked to Dr. Fisher's office and explained to the receptionist what had happened. When the nurse asked to see my wounds, I lifted my dress. I still remember the sound of the room gasping. The nurse rushed me straight back to the doctor for urgent care.

That experience stayed with me. It wasn't just the injury—it was the abandonment. That pattern of neglect repeated itself over and over.

Another time, I had been climbing a rope in the yard when it snapped. I fell hard onto some bricks and had the wind knocked out of me. I was only eight years old and could barely breathe. I managed to get up and ran home, terrified and in tears.

I ran to my mother, hoping for comfort. She laughed in my face.

"What's all the crying for?" she sneered. "Are you too heavy? Did you break the rope because you're fat? Go to your room. I'll put you on a diet. Stop being a baby."

Her words cut deeper than any fall ever could. That moment scared me. Not just the physical pain, but the realization that my mother found my suffering amusing.

Sometimes, I think it would have been better if I had died as a child. Maybe then the rest of the children wouldn't have had to suffer the way I did.

I have countless memories like this. So many that I know I could talk for years and still not finish describing the abuse I endured. My parents—my mother and father—were two of the cruelest people I have ever known.

I remembered another day. I came home from school to find my mother waiting in the car. It was packed with our belongings, and a moving van sat in the driveway.

She told Rodger and me that we were leaving. She was running from our father. We were going to live without him for a while. We moved to Lexington and into a rental house on Olive Court. Rodger and I had no idea what was happening, but Dottie, our housekeeper, did her best to care for us and make sense of the chaos.

Not long after the move, a man moved in with us. My mother called him Uncle Gayle. I believed he was actually our uncle. He was playful and fun, always making us laugh. He shared a room with my mother, though I didn't understand what that meant at the time.

Our time on Olive Court was wild and confusing. I was still enrolled at the girls' school in Versailles, and Rodger was going to school in Midway. Our mornings started very early to make the long drive from Lexington to our schools.

We didn't stay at Olive Court for long. Eventually, my father started courting my mother again, trying to convince her to come back. He promised that if she returned, he would move us to Florida permanently.

And just like that, we were off to Florida again.

CHAPTER 5

A HOUSE WITHOUT SAFETY

I t was the summer of 1966, and I was preparing to enter the fifth grade. My father had secured a job with Florida's Health and Rehabilitative Services in their child welfare department. My mother had been hired to teach fifth grade at a school in Hollywood. She decided that Rodger and I would attend the same school where she worked.

At first, I felt proud. It felt special, almost important, to have my mother as a teacher at my school. But that pride did not last. Very quickly, it turned into embarrassment. Soon after the school year began, my mother started humiliating me in front of her class, my class, and anyone else around.

She had a habit of bringing home children from her work in child welfare, and now she was doing it again—only this time, it was a boy in her classroom. His name was Robbie Straher. He was a handsome ten-year-old boy from Kentucky, and my mother said she felt a special connection to him.

Robbie began spending weekends at our house. My mother showered him with gifts—new bicycles, toys, clothes. I watched in silence, deeply hurt. I felt invisible in my own home. I was forbidden to talk about it or express how I felt. I had a crush on Robbie, and my mother knew it. I think that made it even more entertaining for her. She loved to tease me about it. She would take Robbie and Rodger out on outings and leave me at home. She made comments about how much Robbie liked being with her, as if to rub it in.

Later that year, I developed a crush on another boy named Larry Paton. He was also a student in my mother's fifth grade class. When my mother found out he was interested in me, she told him to forget about it. She said I still wet the bed. I was mortified. She always found new ways to make me feel ashamed, rejected, or unworthy of friendship.

One afternoon, I scraped my knee on the playground and went to find my mother. I was crying, instinctively seeking comfort. I opened the door to her classroom, hoping she would help me. Instead, she turned to me in front of her entire class and said, "Winston, I could hear you crying all the way from the playground. What is your problem? Go see the nurse."

As I turned to leave, humiliated and in pain, I heard her add, "Forgive my daughter. She really isn't very bright. Obviously, she doesn't think."

The class erupted in laughter.

I wanted to disappear. I felt as if the ground could have opened up beneath me, and I would have welcomed it.

If I ever mentioned that I had a good day at school, or if I started to feel the smallest bit of confidence, my mother would find a way to tear it down. She had many methods of cruelty, but there was one moment during that year that damaged me deeply. A moment that still echoes in my mind.

It happened during the ride home from school. Out of nowhere, my mother said to Rodger, "I've seen your IQ scores. They're very high—140. That means you're very bright."

Rodger smiled, but he was too young to understand the weight of what she said.

Then she turned to me.

"Winnie, your scores weren't what I expected, considering you're the child of two intelligent parents. Your IQ was barely average. One twelve. That means you'll have a difficult time learning, and you're definitely not college material."

At the time, I didn't fully grasp what she was saying. But as I grew older, those words shaped the way I saw myself. I believed I was slow, not smart enough, not capable.

That statement caused me years of self-doubt. I internalized it. I lived it.

My fifth-grade year became the beginning of my academic decline. To this day, my parents have no idea why I struggled in school. And if I ever brought it up, my mother would either deny saying those things or claim she meant to motivate me.

In one therapy session, I screamed out loud, "Mom, do you remember telling me about my low IQ? Of course, you'll deny it. Or you'll say, 'Oh, that's not what I said. I was trying to motivate you.' But I want to tell you, even at thirty-three years old, you never understood what kind of person I was. You never knew how to reach me."

Joan encouraged me. "Good, Laura. Let it out. Tell your mother what you wish you could have said when you were nine or ten years old."

She asked, "Why do you call yourself Winnie or Winston sometimes?"

"My middle name is Winston," I explained. "My mom's name is Laura. So the family started calling me Winnie to avoid confusion, and it just stuck."

After that year, my mother began to spiral. She didn't get a teaching job for the following school year, 1967 to 1968. She sank into a deep depression. She barely got out of bed.

My father, on the other hand, thrived during her decline. While she stayed in bed for months, my father used her illness as a free pass to do whatever he pleased. He went out drinking. He chased other women. He didn't lift a finger to help her or care for us. I believe he hoped she would die. That way, he could inherit her money and live the life he wanted without anyone standing in his way.

He barely came home. If he showed up at all, it was for special occasions like Christmas, and even then, he couldn't stand to be around us for long. To escape, he would start a fight, blame us for being loud or obnoxious, and storm out.

That's what happened on Christmas morning.

He picked a fight and left.

The Christmas before that was just as miserable. My father had wanted to go to Kentucky without us, but my mother insisted we go as a family. He was furious. We didn't know it at the time, but he had plans to help Carol Bond move from Kentucky to Florida. Our presence ruined those plans, and he made us suffer for it during the long, exhausting car ride.

The following year, as my mother sank deeper into her depression, Carol was waiting. Waiting for my mother to give up. Waiting for her to die so she could take her place and marry my father..

While my mother lay in bed, gripped by depression, and Carol stood by, patiently waiting for her to die so she could take her place, my father had already moved on to a third woman. Her name was Allison. She was a nineteen-year-old secretary he had met at work. Tall, blonde, and naive, she was easily charmed by my father's polished appearance and carefully rehearsed sob stories. To her, he was a knight in shining armor—an older, good-looking man who claimed to be trapped in a loveless marriage, mistreated by his cruel wife, and tormented by unruly children. He said he wanted out, but didn't know how.

While my mother withered in sickness, while Carol harassed him with fantasies of marriage, Allison was offering sympathy, admiration, and wide-eyed attention. My father was in his element. He was thriving in the center of this chaos, spinning lies and juggling women, all while his own family unraveled. It was pathetic, but to him, it was power.

The one thing he hadn't counted on was our next-door neighbor, Penny Lapitz. Penny saw what was happening and, unlike everyone else, chose to act. She took my mother to see a doctor. That doctor, Dr. Snedeker, was kind and attentive. He listened to my mother and prescribed her Dexedrine to help lift her mood. What he didn't know was that my mother's depression was layered beneath years of unresolved trauma and abusive tendencies of her own.

The medication sent her spiraling.

Instead of helping, it made her volatile. She began to lash out at us violently, both physically and emotionally. Her rages were intense, often fueled by the belief that it was our fault my father didn't come home. She said we were too loud, too wild, too much. We became the scapegoats for her pain, and soon we believed we were the cause of their crumbling marriage.

My mother, still consumed by anger and humiliation over my father's infidelity, would force me to admit what I didn't want to believe. She beat me until I said the words she wanted to hear: that my father was a no-good son of a bitch. It didn't matter what I believed. I had to confess or suffer the consequences.

But soon, she wouldn't have to try so hard. Fate decided to intervene.

One afternoon, my mother took us to the beach. She brought along her friend, Pat Holiday, a woman I liked because she was kind and often acted as a buffer when my mother became aggressive. That day at the beach had been peaceful. We felt safe. That was rare.

But as we drove home, everything changed. As we passed the Parrot Lounge, a popular local bar, we saw a familiar car in the parking lot. It was my father's convertible Cadillac. He was sitting inside it, putting the top up. Next to him was a young blonde woman. Allison.

She didn't even look away when she saw us. She didn't seem embarrassed or ashamed to be caught sitting beside a married man, surrounded by his children.

My mother lost control.

We pulled up alongside the car, and my father rolled down his window. With the smugness only he could summon in such a moment, he looked at my mother and said, "What the hell are you doing here, you bitch? Why are you following me?"

I watched my mother break. She screamed and cried. Pat tried to calm her down and took us all home. Rodger and I sat in the backseat, shaken and silent.

That night, we waited, knowing what was coming. We waited for my father to come home, to start the inevitable fight. We waited for him to twist the story and somehow blame us for what he had done.

And he did.

He told my mother that Allison understood him in ways we never could. That she listened. That life with us was unbearable. That we were too loud, too messy, too difficult. He never took responsibility. Not once.

But this time, something shifted in my mother. The humiliation had reached a breaking point. She sought out an attorney to begin the process of divorce. My father had no idea. He thought he still had time. He believed he could continue playing the same game, scaring us into silence, manipulating emotions, vanishing for days, and returning whenever he pleased. He moved in with Allison and lived as though he had nothing to lose.

What he didn't know was that the attorney my mother spoke to had taken pity on her. According to her, he told my mother plainly that if she stayed married to this man, Rodger would end up in jail and I would grow up to become a prostitute. That was all my mother needed to hear.

She came home with fire in her eyes and announced that she was finally going to ask my father to leave.

That same day, my father pulled his usual routine. He asked Rodger and me to wash and wax his car. He promised us ice cream afterward. It was a lie we had heard a dozen times. We knew what it meant. It meant he had a date.

We went along with it anyway. After we finished, he told us he just had a quick errand to run and that we'd get our ice cream when he returned. But he didn't come back that night. Or the next. We never got the ice cream. We never did.

My father became bolder in the final days of their marriage. He strutted through life like nothing could touch him. Meanwhile, Carol—his country girlfriend—was growing more impatient. In a desperate move, she started calling our house, demanding to know where he was. She would scream, threaten to kill herself, beg for answers.

My mother would locate my father, pass along the message, and he would come home furious—not at Carol, but at my mother. He said she was interfering. Interrupting. Ruining his time with Allison.

The walls were closing in. The lifestyle he had enjoyed, funded by my mother's work and stolen through lies and manipulation, was falling apart.

Then it happened.

One night, my father stormed into the house, shouting that he had been served divorce papers at work. He was livid. He told my mother that she had no idea what kind of predicament she had put him in. Now he would be forced to marry Allison. He was losing control, and he hated it.

The shouting turned into rage. The rage turned into something worse.

I was in my room when I heard the screaming. I came out and saw my father in his blue-striped nightshirt. His underwear was around his ankles. He was on top of my mother. She was kicking and crying and trying to fight him off.

He was raping her.

I stood frozen. I didn't know what to do. I didn't know how to stop him. So I went back to my room. I lay down and cried.

I never told anyone. I didn't speak about it. I held it in.

That's what I had learned to do with trauma. Bury it. Swallow it. Lock it inside.

But what I didn't know then was that the silence, the holding in, would become part of my undoing. It would grow into something that would haunt me for years.

Something I would carry until my body and mind could no longer carry it alone.

CHAPTER 6

THE BREAKING POINT

T he next morning, my mother told my father to leave the house for good. She was done. No more second chances, no more hoping he'd change. But my father, in all his self-assured arrogance, believed she would come crawling back. He assumed he had gotten her pregnant and that eventually, she would call him, beg him to return, and everything would go back to how it had been. In the meantime, he chose to celebrate what he saw as a new lease on life. He rented an apartment and resumed his life of lies, juggling his multiple girlfriends without a shred of guilt.

I later learned that he had been telling Allison he planned to marry her, while also telling Carol she was the one. He was manipulating both women. But before tying himself down, he figured he needed to get back into my mother's good graces—long enough to secure some kind of financial advantage. He wanted to walk away from the marriage with more than he brought in.

But fate turned the tables on him.

My mother wasn't pregnant.

Allison was.

She had already left the job where she and my father met and had moved on to working as a legal secretary for a powerful attorney in Fort Lauderdale. When the divorce between my parents didn't progress quickly enough, Allison began to lose her patience. She used her connections—her boss and a friendly judge—to push the divorce forward.

That's when my father began to panic.

Now, it looked like he would have to marry Allison for real—and it was far from the fantasy he had imagined. Allison came from nothing. She had no education, no financial security, and no family wealth. Her father had died young, leaving her mother, Jane, to raise three daughters on her own. My mother even speculated that Allison might be the teenage mother of her supposed younger sister, Betty—who was actually younger than I was, and I was only twelve.

The first time I ever met Allison in person was one of those unforgettable moments when my father made it painfully clear how little he valued my emotional well-being.

After the separation, my mother insisted that he take us out on weekends. One Saturday, he picked me up alone. Rodger had refused to go. I felt nervous, unsettled.

"Where are we going?" I asked.

"To a picnic," he replied casually.

When we arrived at a house I didn't recognize, I asked,

"Whose house is this?"

He told me to be quiet, come inside, and try not to cause trouble. I asked again about the picnic, but he ignored me.

Inside, we were greeted by an older woman named Jane, who smiled and welcomed us like we were family. Everyone in the house seemed to know and adore my father. I felt like a ghost. I just stood there, observing, feeling out of place.

Then, he introduced me to a tall blonde woman. "This is Allison," he said.

No explanation. No preparation. No sensitivity.

He introduced me to his girlfriend, a woman he had been cheating with, while he was still married to my mother—and then left me there alone to interact with these strangers. I was a child. There was no picnic. That had been a lie.

I left that day feeling gutted. I just wanted to go home.

But the cruelty didn't end there.

Sometime later, he invited me to his bachelor apartment. I thought maybe he wanted to make things right. Instead, it became another chapter in the ongoing abuse.

We went swimming in the apartment complex pool. A while later, Allison arrived in an orange bathing suit. I remember staring at the moles that covered her upper chest. She didn't smile. She barely spoke. She looked at me like I was a threat—like I was my father's problem that she'd have to tolerate.

She left shortly after.

Then my father and I went upstairs to change. I was in the bathroom, with my bathing suit bottoms off, when he walked in without knocking.

He reached out and stroked my labia.

He laughed and said he was just checking to see if I had pubic hair yet.

I froze. Then I cried. I felt physically ill. I didn't understand the full depth of what had happened, but I knew something was very, very wrong. I promised myself that day I would never be alone with him again.

And I've kept that promise ever since.

Later, when I had the courage to speak about what happened, he denied it. He said I was making it up. But I know what he did. I know what it felt like. And even though there was no penetration, he violated me. He crossed a sacred line that no parent should ever come close to.

This was not an isolated incident.

He had mistreated me for most of my life.

One of his favorite games was to chase me, pin me to the floor with his full body weight—he was over one hundred seventy pounds—and tickle me until I couldn't breathe. I would laugh and cry at the same time, begging him to stop, gasping for air.

He thought it was hilarious.

When I cried, really cried, he got angry. He'd call me a crybaby and punish me for being "too sensitive." I was sent to my room like I had done something wrong.

He also loved to frighten us. He would make up stories about monsters in the garage, or tell us he was going to lock us in the dark. One of the worst nights was when I was forced to go outside and turn off the pool filter. It was pitch black. My parents knew how scared I was of the dark, which only encouraged them to make it worse.

My brother's window overlooked the pool. It was open.

Just as I flipped the switch to turn off the filter, my parents screamed "boooo!" in unison. Loud, distorted, monstrous voices.

I panicked. I lost control. I ran toward the house, sobbing and trembling. In my hysteria, I tripped and fell into the shallow end of the pool.

I lay there shaking.

They stood at the window laughing. They called me stupid.

Another time, I was sleeping in—probably depressed—and didn't get out of bed until almost noon. They decided to play a prank. They crept into my room, picked me up while I slept, and carried me to the pool.

I woke up the moment my body hit the water.

I gasped, inhaled water, and surfaced coughing and crying. My light pink nightgown clung to my body. My breasts and pubic hair were visible through the soaked fabric.

They stood there laughing.

Then they walked back inside and left me alone.

If they weren't beating each other or hitting us, their favorite pastime was terrorizing their children.

Their divorce was finalized when I was thirteen years old. But it didn't end the abuse.

It just changed its shape.

To this day, they claim I misinterpreted everything. That I'm exaggerating. That I'm confused.

And I always ask them, "What do I possibly gain by making this up?"

I don't tell many people these things. It's too hard. Too heavy.

And I've stopped trying to get empathy from them. I've stopped hoping for an apology.

I know they will go to their graves denying everything.

But I won't.

I know what happened.

And I will never forget.

CHAPTER 7

SHADOWS OF THE PAST

The sad part of the whole miserable story is that their legacy of sickness will continue on into two more generations. My brother did not make it, but my sister, Ruth, has had four children. She abandoned the two from her first marriage. Their names are David and Dawn. Both of them are already showing the usual signs of being in emotional trouble. But my sister, like my parents, will stay in her comfortable world of substance abuse and will not attempt to do anything to save her children. My parents have always behaved like children are expendable, and my sister continues the legacy.

Her other two children are boys, Derek and Don. The older one is three and already mimicking his cop father's behavior by calling women "cunts" and hating "projects." The second husband of my sister just fits right into the family abuse cycle. Just as predictable as we all are to die, here he comes—with all his cop might and brawn—and clobbers my sister very early into their relationship. And of course, what does Ruth do? She marries him.

Why?

Ruth married him because she has not realized that sexual intercourse can lead to pregnancy. So here comes the bride and the baby—and another child born into the family sickness.

My sister's husband, of course, has been able to stay on as a police officer with the Oakland Park Police Department. Typically, he was promoted and given the okay to continue his racist, bigoted behavior. He is given a license to have more abusive interludes with my sister. Ruth is impaired both intellectually and emotionally and has decided her answer to survival is booze, marijuana, prescription drugs, crack, crank—and having two more babies.

My mother's abusive behavior became more dangerous and destructive after my father left the house. Dad was forced to marry the woman he impregnated by friendly coercion from Allison's influential legal friends. The whole time, my father would come over to our house and blame our mother for coercing him to have to marry "that bimbo."

My siblings and I were not invited to my father's second, third, fourth, or fifth wedding, but not being invited to his marriage to his second wife was hurtful. By the time he married for the third, fourth, and fifth times, we were all okay with no invitation. My mother did rub it in that we were not invited to my father's second wedding, but my mother never forced my father to do the right thing.

Later down the road, my father would use this against her. He said that because my mother never forced him to take responsibility, that was the reason why he was not a good parent to me, Rodger, or Ruth, and why he was a better parent to his daughter by Allison. Her name is Janie.

My father was so busy setting up house with this new wife and baby that we saw him less and less. My mother became meaner and crueler every day. She told me soon after Dad left that if it seemed like she took things out on me more than she should, it was because of my unfortunate stroke of luck of looking just like my father.

Even armed with this information, I was not able to understand her motives or save myself from her rages and outbursts that were directed at me for all the years to come.

My mother has always denied telling me that she picked on me more because I looked like my father. But she told me this when I was thirteen years old, while she and I were in the car. Why and how could I make that statement up? What kid would even think of that?

The death of my brother Rodger had a significant impact on me when it came to verifying certain events. You see, Rodger and I were the only two who could state for a fact—and verify with each other—that yes, indeed, our father and mother did and said things that they can now easily deny.

That is why the death of my brother has been easier for both my parents to handle than it is for other parents who have lost a child. My parents both realized that with Rodger gone, it was virtually my word against theirs when it came to my allegations of child abuse.

My father and his wife, Allison, lived about five miles from us. He hardly ever came by to see us. He never paid his court-ordered child support, even though he was employed in the child welfare department of Health And Rehabilitative Services. One time, a judge embarrassed my father in court when he was over $9,000.00 in arrears. The judge asked my father how he could be employed as an advocate for children and yet abandon his own.

Dad's life appeared to be running more smoothly than what we were experiencing at my mother's house. During my mother's rages, I would call Dad for help or intervention. But he would never come. This pattern—me calling my dad and him refusing to show up—continued well into my later teen years.

I do remember one time he did come by, but it wasn't to help. It was to badmouth my mother and ask Rodger and me if we had any food to feed him because he had the munchies from smoking marijuana. That was real funny to him. He laughed and joked about how disgusting the house was and how terrible our mother was. When my mother came home that evening, my father assaulted her, and she called the police. We didn't hear from my dad again for a while.

Occasionally, he would call to ask if my younger sister, Ruth, could accompany him, Allison, and Janie to Disney World—but he would never ask about Rodger or me. When I asked my mother why he didn't invite us, she said, "Your father likes to appear young." Rodger and I were too old. Taking us would give away his age. Ruth and Janie were still just babies, and Dad could pass them off as his children from his twenties.

My father never took Rodger or me anywhere again after the divorce. He came around so infrequently that I eventually forgot I even had a father—and that was just fine with him.

In the meantime, my mother had her own wild oats to sow. She met the sister of her friend, Michelle, and the three of them started to hang out together constantly. My mom would work from 9:00 to 5:00, then maybe—or maybe not—prepare us dinner. By 6:00 PM, she was out the door to go party with her friends and wouldn't come home until 6:00 AM the following morning.

During this phase of my mother's partying, all three of us kids were left alone every night. We never knew what time she would come home. We were just petrified the entire night.

My mother found her refuge in being away from her children, so I virtually raised Ruth on my own. The long, lonely, misdirected nights became a haven for three children who needed to entertain themselves. We made up games, but most of the time we fought—badly—and we literally tore up the house.

My mother never cleaned, so we lived in filth and disaster. The garbage piled up in the garage and attracted rats. Every night, Rodger and I would hear noises on the roof. We thought someone was trying to break in. One night it got so loud that we called the police. They came, but they laughed at us for being paranoid. I look back now and wish the cop had taken a closer look at where our parents were. Today, that would not have been ignored.

So many nights we were left to fend for ourselves when it came to food. There was rarely anything in the house, so I often made us egg noodles with butter. My mother did buy food, but she locked it in her bedroom. All the fresh fruit—plums, grapes—and sodas were completely off-limits to us. Eventually, she put a bolt lock on her door after we figured out how to open it.

Our house was located in a very nice neighborhood in Ft. Lauderdale, but because of my parents, I was ostracized by the neighbors. The house was filthy, and no one wanted their kids associating with us. I guess I can't blame them—but if even one of them had tried to intervene, maybe things would have been different. But no one did. They just treated us badly.

School wasn't any better. The kids were just as cruel.

I remember Mrs. Conlin, who lived across the street, approaching me one morning while I was riding my bike. She asked why I didn't take my younger sister to get her hair cut. That neighbor should have gone to my mother, but she didn't like my mother, so she handed the burden to me.

I was eleven years old. My sister Ruth was four.

Ruth was a sickly and underweight child. She had chronic bronchitis and her care was completely neglected by my mother. At the time, our mother was suffering from chronic depression when she wasn't out partying. Ruth just existed. Her hair had become so matted it was a disgrace. She always wore mismatched clothes because she dressed herself. Her diet consisted mostly of 7-Eleven Icees that she would get when our mother decided to get out of bed and make a fast food run.

I stole eight dollars from my mother's wallet, put Ruth on my bike, and took her to get her hair cut. The barber ended up cutting most of it off. It was a cute cut, and Ruth looked much better afterward. But the neglect would continue for most of her life.

Ruth was not abused as emotionally or physically as I was—but she was severely neglected.

That's why school situation began to deteriorate in the eighth grade. I found it very hard to stay awake all night. With being mistreated so badly and then being made fun of at school, I began acting out by shoplifting. I did this for a year and was very good at it. I never got caught until my buddy Marlene's parents found out and brought it to my mother's attention. My mother just put the items I had stolen into her drawer, and I eventually stole them back from her.

During those long nights without supervision, Rodger and I became emotionally unmoored. One night, in a state of confusion and sadness neither of us understood, we crossed a line that should never have been crossed. We were children, navigating trauma without guidance. What happened that night left us with a shame we never talked about again. It altered our bond forever. I still feel sick thinking about how much pain we were in to seek connection in such a broken way. This still captures the gravity of what occurred. It does not excuse or erase. But it shifts the focus from specific physical detail to emotional consequence and childhood vulnerability.

My mother cared about us less and less and stayed away longer and longer. She had no idea what was happening to Rodger and me, nor did she care. I started skipping school. With my reputation of being from a horrible family, the guys started to taunt me and I started to like the attention. I fooled around with several school kids and my reputation was forever destroyed. But I had it coming. I felt like a piece of crap. The only solace I had was in my animals.

I had a cat named Anastasia and a dog named Ricky. Anastasia became pregnant and had kittens, so now I had a family. I tormented my dog by teasing him and I am so sorry now, but I was taking out my anger on my dog and I did not even realize it. I thought I loved him.

Well, one day I came home from school and all my cats were gone. I could not believe it, so I called my mother at work. She said to me, "Oh, so sorry, we got rid of them, so live with it." She said she and her friend, who we called Uncle Gayle, had taken them to a farm.

This incident began my first spiral of decline into a clinical depression. My mother had just taken from me, without any regard to my feelings, the three animals that I loved and had been able to show affection to. The affection I gave to those cats helped me cope with daily horror, and they were just ripped out of my heart. My mother to this day does not understand the hurt she caused. Or maybe she does not see what she did as cruel by taking away something I cared about. I will never know the answer. I was so devastated.

This was the first time I had ever thought about dying at my own hands. I was thirteen years old. My God, I look back and think how sick and destructive an environment it must have been for a thirteen-year-old child to think of suicide. I cry for myself when I remember these events. I put a plastic laundry bag over my head and tried to suffocate myself. But I could not do it.

So I began my life of entirely destructive behavior, because I now hated myself. I knew I was all alone in this world, with not a soul to look after my best interests.

CHAPTER 8

THE COST OF SILENCE

My mother's friend Gayle was thirty-two years old and took full advantage of my hatred for her. He used it for his own benefit. Over the course of several days, he seduced me—carefully, manipulatively—until I finally begged him to stop. I was too young, too broken, and too emotionally unstable to understand what was really happening. Eventually, I turned his attention toward a girlfriend of mine who was more sexually active. Only then did he finally leave me alone.

Eventually, Gayle went back to Kentucky. I was left feeling hollow and used. I fell into a deeper depression and became easy prey for men. One night at the roller rink, a sick guy named Richey Henney seduced me. I had already lost any sense of self-worth. Now, I was on a path of no self-respect.

Still, I trudged along. I kept trying to get up and go to school. By this time, I was finishing my freshman year of high school.

One afternoon, I felt incredibly nauseous. I vomited in front of a friend. Embarrassed, I told her I had missed my period. She told me I could be pregnant and said I'd better tell my mother.

Somehow, I gathered enough strength to tell my mother I might be pregnant. I'm not sure if I told her because I was desperate for help, or if, on some level, I wanted to hurt her with the news. Maybe it was both. Regardless, her response was predictable—she called everyone.

She told my father. She told her two best friends. When my dad's ex-girlfriend Carol Bond called, she told her too. Then Gayle knew. Then Ellie. Then her coworkers. And so on. I was devastated. Humiliated. Completely exposed.

Then my father's wife called and offered to help. I thought to myself, "This woman got herself knocked up by my dad while he was still married to my mother—and she thinks I want her advice?"

Next, my father stormed into our house with his accusatory tone, pointing at me, screaming at my mother, "Are you sure she's pregnant? How did you let this happen?" They fought bitterly, blaming each other for what had happened to me. Then he turned on me.

He called me a whore. A slut. He yelled about how he would now have to sell his boat just to pay for me to go to New York to get an abortion. In 1972, abortion was only legal in New York. This was a man who had never paid child support. A man who never showed up or cared what happened in our lives. And now he wanted to judge me?

I will never forget this experience. If I thought things were already bad in my life, this was the moment when I learned just how cruel the world could really be. The tragedy was, I had never been taught how to deal with cruelty or adversity. I had never experienced love, so my abortion—something already traumatic—became a horrifying lesson in human cruelty.

My father and mother managed to come up with the money to take me to New York. But my father wouldn't help me in any other way. My mother took me first to see Dr. Donoway, who had replaced our family doctor, Dr. Snedeker, after he passed away.

Dr. Donoway was completely unhinged. He was judgmental and cold. He didn't ask how I ended up in this situation. He didn't ask if I was okay. He just made the arrangements to get us to New York.

I remember sitting on the plane, staring out the window, thinking about how excited I was to be going to the city where Buffy and Jodie lived on the sitcom *Family Affair*. It sounds pathetic now, but I was still a child. I had no real understanding of the gravity of what had happened to me or what was about to happen.

We arrived at the hotel and went to bed early. My surgery was scheduled for early the next morning.

We took a cab to Flushing Hospital. When we arrived, I was brought into a clinic. A man I assumed was a doctor—looking back, he was probably a resident—told me flatly to remove the bottom half of my clothing. He said he had to do a pelvic exam. I had no idea what that meant.

My mother left me alone. The resident treated me with disgust and cold detachment. He never explained what he was doing or what I should expect. He inserted the speculum cold, hard, and fast. The pain made me cry out, but worse than the pain was the humiliation. I felt completely violated.

He told me to calm down or the hospital wouldn't help me.

Next, I was taken to the operating room waiting area where I experienced my first IV insertion. Three nurses each tried three times to find a vein. Then two anesthesiologists tried—twice each. Finally, a nurse in the operating room was able to insert a butterfly needle and administer the anesthesia.

I had been stuck fifteen times in total.

No one treated me like a young patient. No one offered comfort. I even overheard one nurse telling her supervisor that she refused to care for me because of her religious beliefs as a Catholic and because I was having an elective abortion. I didn't understand the full meaning of what she said at the time. But later, as a nurse myself, I would remember every detail of what happened to me that day.

To this day, I have never witnessed more cruelty from a medical staff than what I experienced at Flushing Hospital in the fall of 1971.

I woke up in the early afternoon. The procedure was over. I was cramping, but physically okay. My mother and I flew home and never spoke about it again.

But I still had one last follow-up appointment—with the dreadful Dr. Donoway. My mother refused to take me. I had to ride the bus alone.

I didn't know I would have to endure another pelvic exam. When I left the doctor's office, I sat crying on the curb, waiting for the city bus to take me home—violated again, alone again.

CHAPTER 9

PERMISSION TO DISAPPEAR

S chool was ending, and I remember thinking how relieved I was. I just didn't feel up to returning for more of the usual taunts and teasing from the kids. That summer, Lorna moved into our house. She was the sister of my mother's friend, Michelle. Lorna was only about twenty-one and had come to Florida from Virginia looking for fun in Ft. Lauderdale—the ultimate party town.

For my mom, it was perfect. She now had a built-in party partner. The two of them did everything together. They partied together, went out to dinner together, and even slept in the same bed for over two years. Naturally, I was jealous of their relationship. My mother treated Lorna better than she treated me. She gave Lorna nicer gifts for birthdays and Christmas. I think I first noticed this difference in treatment when I was about ten years old, back when she favored that boy from her fifth-grade class in eastern Kentucky over her own daughter.

She treated my father better, too. For example, on Saturdays when we'd be swimming, she'd make peanut butter sandwiches for Rodger and me, but serve my dad sliced steak sandwiches. We always got less, and even when I asked for more, I knew better than to ask for a steak sandwich. It may seem trivial, but moments like those added to the growing sense of worthlessness that I was carrying.

Lorna was a terrible person. She had no love in her and no values. Just like my mother, she was disturbed and selfish. She made it very clear to Rodger and me that she had no patience for "bratty kids." She would stay out all night and sleep all day. We were constantly told by her and my mother to keep quiet. Eventually, Lorna, Mom, and Michelle started bringing their male "friends" home. Sometimes they even shared the same guy, sleeping with him in my mother's bed.

One night, the three of them came home late after partying—on a school night. I remember hearing them come in, laughing, blasting music, making no effort to be quiet even though three school-aged children were asleep in the house. I overheard my mom say she'd run out of liquor and would be right back. She left Josie and two men in the house.

One of the men found his way into my sister's bedroom, walked through our adjoining bathroom, and urinated there. Then he came into my bedroom and jumped on top of me. I screamed. Rodger ran into my room to help me, and the man fled. When I told my mother what happened, she didn't believe me. As usual.

The incidents kept happening, one after another. I began to slip into a deeper depression. By the time school started, I was a completely different person. That year, I bought clothes no self-respecting fifteen-year-old should wear—hot pants and boots, clothes that reflected exactly what I thought of myself. I felt like a toy for men and boys.

I had no self-respect.

I started experimenting with drugs and stayed away from home as often as I could. My mother never asked where I was. As long as I didn't bother her, she didn't care. She even started paying Ruth, who was now eight, twenty dollars to "get lost" for the entire day. Ruth would be gone from morning until night. The neighbors started calling her the orphan. Not that anyone cared enough to intervene.

So much for the divorce making things better. If anything, our lives became even more unstable and dangerous. My mother grew more abusive, more neglectful. She would remind me over and over that because I looked like my father, she took things out on me more than the others.

And I grew angrier and angrier.

By the time I was fifteen, I had started stealing my mother's car. She would come home around six in the morning after partying all night and collapse in bed. I would sneak the car out of the driveway and cruise around

Ft. Lauderdale until it was time for school. Most of the time, I skipped school entirely. Nobody cared.

Then my mother met a man. His name was Brian Mase. They started dating regularly, and she told me that she thought he might be the kind of man who could help her become a good mother because he was a good man. I was actually excited to meet him. Brian was a sergeant with the local police department, and I liked him right away.

That Christmas, when I turned sixteen, I received a 1962 Volkswagen Beetle as a present from my mother and Brian. I was over the moon. It was the most remarkable gift I had ever received, especially considering how the past ten years had been. I couldn't believe it. I finally had transportation. I was truly happy for once.

But, of course, the happiness didn't last.

A few days later, I was driving around the Oakland Park area when a police officer pulled me over. I heard him speak through the bullhorn, asking me to step out of the vehicle. Terrified and confused, I did as he said. I had no idea why I had been stopped.

Then the officer got out of his vehicle—and it was Brian.

I burst into laughter, overwhelmed with relief. Brian laughed too. We talked for a few minutes, and then I drove off. But just as I pulled back onto the boulevard, blue lights flashed behind me again. Another officer.

I pulled over, still thinking it was Brian playing another joke. I got out laughing and called out, "Okay, Brian, give it a rest."

But it wasn't Brian.

It was another officer entirely. He looked at me and asked if I knew who he was. Still laughing, I said, "I thought you were my mother's boyfriend, Brian Mase." The officer replied, "Oh, your mother's boyfriend? Well, any friend of Brian's is a friend of mine. I pulled you over for going too slow. So go on home now and tell Brian I said hello."

I smiled and said I would. Then I drove home, excited to tell Brian and my mother about the whole thing.

However, when I returned home that day, I heard my mother crying and screaming at Brian over the phone. As soon as she saw me, she ended the call, telling him she would call him back later. I had no idea what was coming next.

She came at me in a rage. Without saying a word, she struck me across the face and began beating the living hell out of me before I could even understand why. I had long hair, and she yanked at it so hard I thought it would rip from my scalp. I ran into my brother's bathroom and tried to hold the shower doors closed to protect myself. But she forced them open, grabbed me by the hair, and slammed my head into the tiled wall, all while screaming that I was an ungrateful bitch.

The assault continued into my bedroom. I tried hiding beside my bed, shielding my head with my arms, but that only left my back exposed. My mother saw the bookshelf near my door, grabbed every hardback book she could, and began throwing them at me. One of them, my Girl Scout manual, sliced open my back.

Still not done, she chased me into the den, knocked me to the ground, and jumped on me. I heard something crack in my spine. My mother was not a small woman—she weighed around 250 pounds—and the weight of her body only made it worse.

Something inside me snapped. I ran back to the bathroom, hiding under the shower again, desperate to escape. Rodger heard the chaos and rushed in. He turned on the water and screamed at our mother to stop. Only then did she back away and begin walking toward her bedroom. But I was beyond reason at that point. I was so angry, so overwhelmed with rage, that I went after her. I truly believe I could have killed my mother that night.

Later, I found out what triggered her fury. She had been seeing a married man—Brian—and when I was pulled over by the police, I had told the officer I thought he was Brian. That information got back to Brian's superiors. He was demoted for violating department policy, and my mother blamed me entirely for the fallout.

The next thing I knew, I came home from school and my bags were packed. My mother handed me a one-way bus ticket to Kentucky and told me I was leaving the next day. She said she was worried I might act out and try to seduce Brian since, in her words, I had already "proven what a whore" I was.

That night, something inside me died.

I begged her to let me stay. It was December, my senior year. I didn't know how I would finish high school. But she didn't care. She drove me to the Greyhound bus station, handed me the ticket, and placed me on a bus bound for Lexington, Kentucky. She told me my grandmother Ruth would be waiting when I arrived.

I got to Lexington around 11:00 PM and was told I would have to wait until 6:00 AM for a connecting bus to Midway, where my grandmother lived. It was freezing cold, and my mother hadn't even packed a coat.

But a small stroke of luck came my way. A Greyhound driver heading home to Frankfort offered to drop me off in Midway. I was relieved—until he started flirting with me. Not long into the ride, he grabbed me and said he wanted to fool around. I screamed. He threw me and my belongings out of the vehicle onto the roadside. Thankfully, we were near Midway. I gathered my things and walked, freezing and coatless, through the night.

As I approached the alley near my grandmother's house, she heard my footsteps and turned on the porch light. When she saw me, she panicked.

"What on earth are you doing here in the middle of the night?" she asked.

I was confused. "Didn't my mother call to tell you I was coming?"

She hadn't. My grandmother didn't know I was coming. She brought me inside right away and tried to call my mother, but the number had been changed. My mother had abandoned me, and she made sure I had no way to reach her.

That hurt more than anything else. I had been thrown out of my home and wasn't even given the chance to call my mother. I remember thinking she might be the cruelest woman alive.

Funny thing was, once I settled in Midway, I started to thrive. Someone finally cared about me. Under my grandmother's roof, I began to do better. In Ft. Lauderdale, I had been failing school. In Midway, I started getting straight A's.

But I was still carrying a massive amount of pain.

Not long after arriving, I took an overdose of my grandmother's medicine. I woke up three days later in the hospital. There, I met a kind nurse who helped clean me up and prepare me for the psychiatrist who was scheduled to see me. His name was Dr. Roach, a long-time family physician. When he came in, he looked at me and said gently, "Laura, what on earth has been going on in Florida?"

And I broke down. I cried for what felt like forever.

That moment in the hospital changed everything. While I was in the bathroom, I experienced something I can only describe as spiritual. When I closed the door, a very bright light filled the space, and I felt a wave of comfort and calm. An unseen presence, an entity, spoke to me—not with words I heard aloud, but with words I felt deep inside.

It said, *If you want to survive, you have to understand that you are on your own.*

The moment only lasted seconds, but it changed me forever.

Later, the psychologist came. She was kind. With her help, I recovered enough to be discharged. I went back to my grandmother's house, and as I walked down the alley toward her door, I felt something I hadn't felt in years: alive.

But the sadness returned quickly. Neither of my parents came to visit me in the hospital.

A few days later, my father showed up in Midway. Not out of concern, but to scold me for the suicide attempt. He offered no compassion. And I never heard from my mother again.

Not long after the suicide attempt, I returned to Ft. Lauderdale. I was genuinely excited to go home, to see my brother, my sister, and my dog Ricky. I took the Greyhound bus and arrived around 10:00 p.m. I grabbed a cab straight to the house.

When I got there, Rodger was at the door and looked horrified to see me. He told me I couldn't come in.

"Why not?" I asked, confused.

"Because Mom's not home," he said nervously.

I went inside anyway and walked straight to my room. But when I opened the door, I stopped in my tracks. Everything was gone. My belongings, my clothes, my furniture—everything had vanished. I dropped to my knees and wailed.

Rodger didn't know what to do. He just stood there looking helpless. I asked him, "Whose things are in my room? Where's all my stuff?"

He told me that the day after I left, Brian's mother, Mildred, had been moved into my room. He had no idea what had happened to my belongings. That night, Rodger and I sat together, got drunk, and played music. There was a new record in the house, and it was beautiful. We listened to it over and over. It was Neil Diamond's *Jonathan Livingston Seagull*. Somehow, that album brought a kind of calm in the middle of the chaos. Funny enough, I still have that album today—on vinyl, cassette, and later on CD. That album got me through some of the worst moments of my life.

Later, I told Joan I was feeling sick just remembering everything. "May I take a break?" I asked.

"Of course, Laura," she said. "Let's call it a day and resume tomorrow at 9 a.m."

That night, the realization of how deeply I'd been abused hit me like a dam breaking. I had never before thought through my past chronologically, nor allowed myself to sit with the full weight of it.

And I couldn't bear it.

That night, I tried to cut my wrists. The nurse came in and bandaged them, and I was put on suicide watch. My medications were changed. I cried alone in my room.

The next morning, I felt physically and emotionally drained. Joan met me in the common room and gently asked me to join her in the conference room. She told me I was working incredibly hard and acknowledged how troubling my background was. She said from this point forward, we would do shorter sessions—because in her entire career, she had never encountered someone with such a history of trauma. She added, "It's amazing that you survived at all." She also suggested bringing my mother in for family counseling, but we agreed to discuss that later.

Then she asked me to pick up where I had left off.

I had just returned to Ft. Lauderdale. Rodger and I were drinking, listening to *Jonathan Livingston Seagull*, and trying to forget everything. Eventually, my mother and Brian came home, having just returned from a trip to Virginia—or so they said. I found out years later that the trip was actually when my mother went for an abortion.

When they walked in, my mother took one look at me and told me to leave immediately. It was 2:00 a.m., and I had nowhere to go. I asked what she'd done with my things, and she told me she had packed everything into my Volkswagen and sent it to my dad's house. I knew that was a lie. My car didn't even run, and none of my belongings had ever shown up. Even my furniture was gone.

I ended up falling asleep behind the house, sobbing in the dark, trying to figure out what to do next.

The next morning, I called my father. He didn't want me either, but reluctantly agreed to let me stay.

At the time, my dad was living with his new wife, Allison, and their daughter Janie, who was now about a year and a half old. It broke my heart to see how loved Janie was. But even in that household, things were chaotic. Allison and Dad fought violently in front of her. The tension in that house made it impossible to relax. Allison hated me. She made it clear I wasn't wanted. Before long, I was told to leave again. I was called "impossible." At that point, I had nowhere else to go. I had no high school diploma, and all my classmates were about to graduate.

I tried to sue my parents for emancipation, but it didn't go anywhere.

Thankfully, my friend Lorraine Cenatiempo and her mother took me in. I stayed with them for a while. I got a job at the local hospital as a transportation aide, and for the first time in a long while, I felt like I had a sense of purpose.

Eventually, my father said he knew a woman—his friend Cindy—who would let me live with her and her daughters while I finished high school. So I moved in. At first, Cindy was good for me. She gave me structure, and I stayed there for about a year. But it turned out she only let me stay because she had a crush on my dad and wanted a connection to him. She didn't realize how little he cared about either of us.

Still, during that time, I earned my GED. Then I applied to the Licensed Practical Nursing (LPN) program at the Vocational Center. While I waited for my acceptance letter, I got promoted at the hospital to phlebotomist. That job trained me in the lab, which would later help tremendously with my nursing career. It also allowed me to buy a car. I was only eighteen and needed a co-signer, so my father agreed to help.

For a moment, I felt like things were finally looking up. I had a job, a car, friends, and a future. I even looked good. For once, I felt happy.

But as always, my happiness was short-lived.

Cindy and my father had a falling out. She found out he was having an affair with a woman at Jordan Marsh, where he worked part-time. I no longer served her purpose, so she kicked me out.

My father, now divorced and living alone, said I could move in with him. When I did, I found some of my things—the ones my mother had told me were gone. I asked Dad how they ended up there. He never admitted it, but I knew. He'd taken them and given them away, then tried to cover it up.

I didn't dwell on it.

I was working full-time and had been accepted to LPN school. I was about to start the next month, and I was excited. I had turned nineteen and, despite everything, I felt like I had come a long way. My life was finally taking shape.

I had become a skilled phlebotomist, and I was even allowed to draw blood from newborns. It was something I was proud of. But one morning, just as I was heading into the nursery for my rounds, the head nurse pulled me aside.

She looked uneasy and asked me to step into the hallway.

"I'm sorry," she said. "Your mother delivered her

baby last night. We have strict orders from her physician that you're not to enter the nursery while she and her baby are here."

I stood frozen. "Why?" I asked.

The nurse leaned in and said, "Confidentially, your mother is afraid you might try to harm her baby."

I could not believe what I was hearing. I stood there stunned, ashamed, and utterly embarrassed. I didn't even know how to respond. I just started crying. I returned to the lab and asked to speak with my supervisor. When I explained what had happened, he saw the state I was in and told me gently, "Go home. Come back tomorrow when you're feeling better." He was one of the kindest people I had ever worked with.

I went home and cried my eyes out. My mother had managed to hurt me again—deeply—despite the fact that I was no longer part of her daily life.

I couldn't understand it. Here I was, trying to overcome a childhood that read like a horror novel, doing everything I could to build a life, to stand on my own, and somehow she still wanted to destroy me. But the truth was, that *was* exactly what she wanted.

When my dad came home that afternoon, he saw me lying in bed crying and asked me why I was being so lazy. Without waiting for an answer, he told me to get up and leave because he was expecting a "friend" over and didn't want me around when she arrived.

So I left. I went to school, even though I was exhausted. I was three-quarters of the way through my LPN program. I was working full-time during the day and attending classes from 3:00 p.m. until 11:00 p.m. every night. I was worn thin. That night, when I came back from school, my father told me I needed to find another place to live because I was interfering with his social life.

By then, I couldn't even react. I was too used to being thrown out. So I complied. I moved in with a friend.

I was starting to feel hopeful again, getting excited

about nearing graduation. But money was tight now that I had to pay rent. Then, while I was working one day, the hospital security guard called me. He said someone was outside repossessing my car.

I was stunned. I ran to the window and saw them hooking it up to a tow truck.

"All of my books are in that car," I said, panicking. "How am I supposed to get to school?"

I called my father immediately to tell him what happened. That's when he told me, casually, that he had received a call from the bank. They asked him to bring the loan current—just two payments of eighty-nine dollars each.

"And I said no," he told me. "I told them to go ahead and repossess it."

I was crushed. He wouldn't even help me when I was trying to help myself.

Of course, this affected my performance at work. I was asked to take some time off. I went home and sat in silence, unable to process how fast everything was unraveling. And that was when it happened—the second time in my life that the light came to me.

That same warm, bright light that had spoken to me once before filled the room again. It told me exactly what to do. I felt it so clearly, as if someone were sitting beside me saying, *"Walk across the street. There are apartments near the hospital. Without the car payment, you can afford to rent a room. You'll be able to walk to work. Start there."*

So I did. I walked across the street and found a small room I could afford. I retrieved my books from the car before they took it away and settled in. I picked up the pieces and moved forward, quietly vowing to never speak to either of my parents again.

And I should have kept that promise.

A few weeks later, I was nearing graduation. I came home one afternoon and found a note taped to my door. It was from the Ft. Lauderdale Police Department. It said to call home. That's how I found out.

My mother's baby—the one she had once told doctors she feared I might harm—was dead. A drowning. They wanted me to attend the funeral.

The funeral was the next day. I had no money and no transportation. My boyfriend at the time, who would later become my husband, offered to take me to the funeral home. I went, like a good and compliant daughter. I didn't know the baby, but I grieved. Not just for the child, but for the loss of any hope that this might soften my mother's heart.

It didn't.

But still, I graduated. I walked across that stage and received my LPN certification. And not long after that, I married John Schneider.

CHAPTER 10

HEALING ON A TIME LIMIT

My therapist, Joan, said that she no longer could handle any more stories. She Joan encouraged me to try to put my past aside for the weekend and attend the hospital barbecue on Saturday. She said I deserved a moment of lightness, a pause from the weight I carried. I agreed, but emotionally, I was still fragile.

That weekend, while I was in the hospital trying to gather the pieces of my life, I found out that my husband—Jack—had decided to take a trip to Boston for a three-day weekend of partying. He had asked me before he left if I minded him going. At the time, I was too numb to think it through. I simply said I didn't care, but that decision stayed with me long after I started to recover. It became painfully clear that Jack valued drinking and spending time with his buddies more than he valued my well-being.

When he called on Monday, I was not ready to speak to him. I was beginning to realize the depth of his detachment. He had withdrawn more money for his three-day trip to Boston than he had given Joshua and me for an entire two-week road trip just a few months earlier.

Jack was always trying to be the big shot. He was constantly influenced by those around him—his father, Jack Sr., their salesman Steve, his mother, and his sister. All of them were telling him to get rid of me. "She's a liability," they said. "Cut your losses before she ruins your life."

Jack would repeat their words to me like he was doing me a favor by staying. But the truth was, he didn't want to help me. He wanted the freedom to drink, party, and keep his perfect image—without the burden of a broken wife he had helped shatter.

That Monday afternoon, I met with a group of women who had survived sexual assaults, many at the hands of people they once trusted. Their stories were gut-wrenchingly familiar. I was angry listening to so many similar stories—stories of betrayal, silence, and denial. I don't believe abuse toward women is increasing; I believe women are finally starting to speak up. With the help of education, the media, and support groups like this one, we finally have a place to speak, to name what happened, and to begin to heal.

Our parents failed us. Instead of preparing us for the world, for men, and for how to protect ourselves, they left us as prey. They denied us protection and denied our pain. And society enabled them. Generation after generation of silence.

After I spoke, the group broke into applause. They said I had captured their feelings in a way that gave voice to the pain they'd buried.

The next day, I was scheduled for another session with Joan. But first, I had to meet with the hospital's financial director and undergo a long list of tests. The weight of depression makes it almost impossible to advocate for yourself, especially in a system eager to exploit your insurance for everything it can.

I was given an EKG, a mammogram, an echocardiogram, an EEG, a CT brain scan, a Pap smear, and other tests I did not even understand. The financial director explained that my in-patient mental health treatment would cost about thirty thousand dollars. Based on her estimates, my portion would be around two thousand.

But twenty-eight days later, when I was discharged, I was informed that my insurance would not be covering anything. I now owed the hospital thirty thousand dollars.

I was shattered.

Jack was livid. Not out of concern for me, but because of the money. That moment cemented what I had always feared: I was on my own. I realized I would need to manage my depressive disorder by myself. I couldn't rely on my parents, who had neglected and damaged me for eighteen years. They weren't going to save me now.

That was another awakening.

So, I went back home and began looking for a job as a nurse. I had hoped to take some time to rest and heal, but Jack was adamant that I start working immediately. He didn't care about my mental health. He cared about income.

I landed a job, but I was still barely holding myself together. For the next three and a half years, I played every role—mother, wife, nurse, maid—without ever tending to my own emotional needs. No one else cared, so I learned to hide my pain. I kept waiting, hoping someone would notice, that someone would care enough to rescue me. But no one ever did.

It was exhausting to exist in a world where I felt so invisible. My son loved me deeply, but he was a child. I was his caretaker, not the other way around. He was my gift, my lifeline. I had brought a beautiful soul into the world, and I was determined not to let my inner torment affect my parenting.

Joshua had only me. I was his one and only parent.

I'll admit—I wasn't always the best mother. I tried. I did the best I could. But parenting without ever having been parented is like being thrown into the ocean and told to swim with no lessons and no life vest. I was learning as I went. And I often failed.

I envied the children who had parents that nurtured them. I used to think to myself: *If only I had been loved, if only I had been supported, I could have been something extraordinary.* I wasn't given a strong start in life—I was set up to be preyed upon. But even still, I gave birth to something extraordinary: my son, Joshua.

He saved me.

Without him, I believe I would have died. He gave me purpose. He grounded me. Loving him allowed me to experience what I had missed. Through nurturing him, I slowly learned how to give and receive love.

But after returning home from the psychiatric hospital, with no outpatient therapy or real support, I began to decline again.

Jack was immature and selfish. He never lightened my burden. He never showed me that he truly cared for me or Joshua. And eventually, my bitterness started spilling onto his son. I hated myself for that. I never wanted to be that person. But I couldn't find it in my heart to care for his son when Jack refused to care for mine—or for me.

I pleaded with Jack to love me better, to try, to care in some way. He told me flatly, "This is as good as it's going to get."

And he meant it.

He became verbally abusive and threatening. He told me that if I ever left him, he would kill me.

CHAPTER 11

LEAVING DOESN'T MEAN YOU'RE FREE

I wanted to leave Jack so badly. I asked myself over and over, "How did I end up in yet another horrible relationship?" It would take me many years to fully understand the answer. But at that moment, the only thing I knew was that I had to get out — quietly and carefully.

I feared what Jack might do if I told him I was leaving. I had seen the anger in him before, and I knew better than to take that risk. So I made a secret plan. I arranged for the moving truck to arrive right after Jack left for work. I had found a small but charming apartment nearby so that

Joshua could stay in the same school. I had thought of everything. I wanted the transition to be as smooth as possible for my son. And in that sense, the move went off without a hitch.

But what I hadn't anticipated was how cruel women could be to each other.

The weight of the move, the stress of rebuilding, and the emotional toll it took on both Joshua and me were overwhelming. He was having a difficult time adjusting, and so was I. And then Jack found out where I had moved. He began calling, begging me to come back.

I was thirty-six years old. Up until then, I had managed to keep my career on track, even through all my personal struggles. But things were beginning to unravel. Slowly. Subtly. Then, all at once.

At the time, I was working in sales and marketing for a home health agency. My depression hovered somewhere between mild and moderate. I dragged myself out of bed every day and wore a perfect mask — the appearance of wellness. No one would have guessed how close I was to breaking.

Then I met Bob. A new surgeon from Pennsylvania. I was excited. Dating again brought a flicker of hope. He told me he was falling in love with me, and that helped me hang on. Bob never knew about the internal war I was fighting, the need I had to stay grounded for the sake of real love. I didn't let him see the cracks.

But once again, I was hurt. Bob had been lying to me all along. He was sexually impotent and deeply insecure. He was threatened by me — by my ambition, by my experience, by my strength. At the time, I didn't realize how much power I held as a woman. I was just someone longing to be loved, looking in all the wrong places.

In the beginning, he did all the romantic things. He sent flowers to my workplace. People admired our relationship from the outside, and that caused envy. Especially from the women I worked with.

There was an LPN at the agency who had always wanted power. She was promoted and placed in a position where, despite my RN credentials, I had to answer to her — a violation of the Florida Nurse Practice Act. I didn't realize just how much she resented me. I was too busy fighting my own battles to see the one brewing around me.

Then came Rachel — another LPN who was hired to "help" in my territory. She was stunning in that conventional way: huge breasts, long blonde hair, and the IQ of a fruit fly. Her first day on the job, she showed up in a skintight, one-piece purple outfit with a bolero jacket and three-inch heels. I was mortified. These were physician offices. This was supposed to be professional. But no one cared. I was told that our boss had a thing for big-breasted women and to just let it go.

It was too much.

Bob had betrayed me. My supervisor wanted to see me fail. My new coworker looked like a centerfold and had no business in the medical field. My mental health started to collapse.

I finally admitted to the LPN manager that I was struggling with depression — a huge act of vulnerability — and she used it against me. This was before the Americans with Disabilities Act existed to protect people like me. Two weeks before Christmas, I was fired because of my illness.

Then they held my final paycheck hostage, claiming I had to return all company property before I could get it. I complied. I went to their lawyer's office and handed over everything. Then they demanded I pay thirty dollars for a phone bill. I didn't have the money. I wrote a check. It bounced.

And that bounced check? It turned into a misdemeanor. A bench warrant was issued for my arrest. I wouldn't find out for eight years.

It was a period of deep humiliation. I had been ambushed by women, abandoned by men, and discarded by the system. I spiraled.

In desperation, I moved to Vero Beach, Florida. I needed a fresh start. My car had been repossessed weeks earlier, so pulling off a relocation while deeply depressed and without transportation felt nearly impossible. But I did it. I found a job and used the offer letter to finance a new car.

It was a sliver of hope.

CHAPTER 12

WHEN HELP TURNS INTO HURT

My car was repossessed because my husband's business had gone into bankruptcy The finance company called in all the loans on the company vehicles—and mine was included. When I called the car dealer to explain my situation, telling him I had just moved, started a new job, and fallen behind on a payment, he showed no sympathy. He took the car back without hesitation. I was devastated. It felt like just another load thrown onto an already unbearable burden. I wanted to die. I didn't want my son to see me this broken, this lost.

For years, Joshua's aunt and uncle, Frank and Julie, had been asking for Joshua to visit them in Pennsylvania. I decided it was time. I reached out and asked if they would be willing to take Joshua for the rest of the school year while I tried to recover from my depression. Frank and Julie agreed immediately. They were thrilled at the chance to have Joshua stay with them and to finally get to know his cousins, Anthony and Antonia.

Joshua was excited too. He had always dreamed of seeing snow and experiencing real winter sports. He was also looking forward to being in a home where a father figure was present. I was grateful to be able to offer him that, even for a little while. Deep down, I knew I couldn't let him see me drowning in my sadness. I didn't want him to be harmed by anything I might say or do in a moment of despair.

Sending Joshua away was the hardest thing I had ever done. He was the most profound reason I had to stay alive. But I kept telling myself—this was the most selfless thing I could do for him.

I put Joshua on that plane in late December 1992. Watching it take off shattered me. I couldn't stop crying. It felt like someone had ripped my heart out and kicked me in the stomach. It was an act of love, but it cost me dearly. I kept trying to remind myself that it was the right thing for him, even though it felt like it was killing me.

I thought I could pull myself together while Joshua was gone, that I could heal quietly and bring him home to a better mother. After he left, I threw myself into finding a new job. I knew I had to get away from Jack—my husband—and Bob—the lying boyfriend who had only made things worse.

I decided to move to Vero Beach, Florida. I began answering classified ads from the newspaper and eventually landed a job as a nurse liaison for a home health agency in Ft. Pierce. It was perfect. I could live in Vero Beach and work nearby. There was just one snag: I had no car.

Desperate, I called Jack and begged for help. After all, he was part of the reason I had lost everything. Jack didn't have any money either, but he promised to find a way to help me secure a vehicle.

I packed up what little I had and moved to Vero Beach with just one thousand dollars to my name. But even that didn't last long. The moving company, seeing I was alone and vulnerable, decided to hold my furniture hostage. They refused to unload it unless I agreed to pay them an extra one thousand dollars in cash. I was so distraught, so desperate, that I wrote them a bad check just to get my belongings back.

Once the movers finally unloaded my furniture, my friend Jennie showed up as planned. She agreed to help me look for a new car. Just down the road from my new place, there was a Mazda dealership. With their help—and the letter of intent from my new job—I managed to buy a brand-new Mazda 626. For the first time in months, I felt a flicker of hope. I thought, *Maybe I'm finally on my way back. Maybe life is about to get back on track.*

But it didn't last.

The job in Ft. Pierce didn't work out. Every weekend, Jack showed up in Vero Beach, begging me to come home. I was still drowning in depression and barely improving at all. Then my grandmother's health began to fail. I didn't want her placed in a nursing home, so Jack agreed to help me. Together, we drove to Kentucky to bring her back to live with me.

It was a hard trip. I had just started seeing a new psychiatrist and had been prescribed Mellaril. During the drive, I developed severe side effects—racing heart, uncontrollable shaking, and terrifying thoughts. I had to stop the medication immediately.

Now, everything was falling apart. I was still deeply depressed. I couldn't tolerate the antidepressants. I missed Joshua terribly, and he missed me just as much. He begged me over the phone to come visit him in Pennsylvania. Meanwhile, my job was miserable, my life felt stuck, and my strength was evaporating.

During this time, I stayed in touch with a male friend named Stephen who lived in New York City. Stephen was kind, but I wasn't interested in him romantically. I told him how much Joshua needed me to visit, and without hesitation, Stephen offered to pay for my flight and hotel.

I didn't hesitate. I needed to see my son.

In February, I flew up to New York. Stephen picked me up at JFK and drove us down to Philadelphia. We stayed at a nice hotel that night, and the next morning, we drove to Holland, Pennsylvania, where Joshua was living with his aunt and uncle.

When we pulled up, everyone came out to greet us. I was so overwhelmed with happiness just to see Joshua that I didn't even notice the tension hanging in the air.

It didn't take long for it to hit me. Frank and Julie treated me terribly. When I finally got Joshua alone, he told me how much he wanted to come home. It broke my heart.

Later, I learned the full extent of what they had been telling him. I had explained to Frank and Julie before sending Joshua that I had lost my job, had my car repossessed, and had moved to Vero Beach to start over after my divorce. I had been honest. But when they saw me arrive in Stephen's $100,000 Mercedes Benz, they made their own assumptions. They decided I was a liar. Worse, they poisoned my son against me. They told Joshua he should never return home because I was a "bad mother."

The truth was, I had sent Joshua away to protect him from my depression. I had tried to do the right thing. But looking back, it's clear—he would have been far better off staying with me.

I couldn't believe the cruelty that existed—not just inside my world, but outside of it too. No one ever really cared about helping me. They were far more interested in believing the worst about me. It didn't help that I had learned how to wear a good facade. I was always nice-looking. Always well-dressed. On the outside, I seemed fine. But inside, I was the walking depressed.

When I returned to Vero Beach, Jack had been staying with my grandmother while I was away. That's when my troubles with her really began. My grandmother Ruth's health was declining fast. Her dementia was worsening, especially at night. She suffered from sundowner's syndrome, which meant that after dark, she became confused, frightened—and sometimes dangerous. More than once, I woke to find her standing over my bed, holding a butcher knife, not recognizing me or remembering where she was.

It became exhausting—and terrifying—to care for her day after day, night after night.

I called my father, her son, and begged him to give me a break. I asked if he could take her for even one weekend now and then. But he refused coldly, telling me, "You made your bed, now lie in it."

I was furious. And when my grandmother had another serious episode that left me fearing for my life, I couldn't do it anymore. I packed her belongings and drove her back to Ft. Lauderdale. I showed up at my father's door and dropped her off.

He wasn't grateful. He wasn't even civil. Instead, he was so angry that he threw a lit cigar in my face.

I turned around, got in my car, and drove away, sobbing so hard I could barely see the road. I couldn't believe the utter disrespect and cruelty I had received at the hands of my own father.

Still desperate for comfort, I decided to drive by my old house to see if Jack was there. I didn't know what else to do. When I arrived, he was home. He welcomed me in and kept begging me to come back. After all my failed attempts to start over on my own, a part of me wondered if maybe—just maybe—I should.

And for the first time in a long while, I said I would give it some serious thought.

∴

CHAPTER 13

WHEN LOVE ISN'T ENOUGH

In the end, I did return to Ft. Lauderdale in April of 1993 to live with my ex-husband. As much as it felt like a defeat, it seemed safer than being alone, exposed, and vulnerable in a world that had proven itself relentlessly cruel. A few weeks later, Joshua came back home, and I slipped into the next phase of my life: seven years of living as a mildly to moderately depressed, but safe, functioning despondent.

Jack had made promises to get me back. He swore he would fix up the house, which had been badly damaged by Hurricane Andrew and further destroyed by four grown men who had lived there like animals. He promised it would be repainted, repaired, and ready for a fresh start.

But when I walked into that house, it was obvious none of it had been done. I stood there, looking at the wreckage, and I broke down in tears. But what choice did I have? I was already back. I was staying—for now.

The house was filthy and in ruins. I grew angrier and angrier at Jack. The truth hit me hard: I could barely stand him anymore. He had lied to me once again. He had no job. He had let the car payment—under my name—fall behind, destroying my credit. It was clear that Jack hadn't wanted me back out of love. He wanted me back so he could continue living off my income. He didn't love me, didn't respect me, and certainly didn't treat me like a wife. To him, my emotional struggles were nothing more than laziness.

I went through the motions. I worked full-time, took care of Joshua, managed the house, cared for our dog and two cats—and managed Jack. He barely worked. After his father's seafood business went bankrupt the previous year, Jack scraped by with odd jobs, earning very little. I became the sole provider for years to come.

Later, Jack finally admitted that during our separation, when he claimed he was working, he had actually been hiding in grocery store parking lots all day, pretending to be at work. He had been too ashamed to tell me he had nothing. This was a healthy, thirty-three-year-old man, fully capable of finding real work. He just chose not to. It was easier to lean on me.

The resentment in me grew deeper. Not only was I supporting him, but he wasn't even kind to me. My only sources of comfort were my son, our dog Tasha, and my swimming pool.

But this time, the trap was tighter. Jack had wrecked my credit. He had let his roommates destroy our home. Joshua was now in high school, and I couldn't uproot him by changing schools this late in the game. I was stuck—at least for the time being.

So, I made a decision. I wasn't going to be trapped forever. I started quietly planning my escape.

I mapped out a seven-year plan. I would rebuild my credit. I would save enough money. I would stabilize everything for Joshua. And I would wait. I knew I was too deeply attached to Tasha, my 110-pound Rottweiler, to ever leave her behind. Apartments that accepted pets like her were almost nonexistent. So I knew I would have to wait until after Tasha's life ended naturally. Only then could I finally walk away clean.

Over those next seven years, I took over our finances completely. I helped Jack build a career. He eventually trained as a cable installer and started to make a decent living—around fifty thousand dollars a year. But I never trusted him with money again. I managed every penny. Jack would hand over his entire paycheck, and I would give him an allowance. It was the only way to keep him from losing or wasting money we didn't have.

Slowly, we climbed out of the mess. It took all of the seven years to repair the house, to rebuild my credit, and to restore some kind of stability. Along the way, Jack's health started to fail too. He suffered from chronic kidney stones, and at one point, both his kidneys became dangerously swollen. He needed surgery—but by then, he had let his insurance lapse without telling me. Paying for that surgery bankrupted my new company. It was another blow in a long line of blows.

Through it all, Jack was a project, a burden. He wasn't a partner. He was a child trapped in a man's body.

We had been married for four years before I left him that first time. When I came back, we never remarried. And during the seven years we lived together again, he never once asked me to. I never brought it up either. Deep down, I knew the truth: we were using each other. He needed someone to support him, and I needed someone to survive with.

But Jack had hurt me more than almost anyone ever had. His neglect, his cruelty, his selfishness—they had almost destroyed me.

And as I stood in that crumbling house, doing everything for everyone once again, I realized that I was surviving, but I wasn't really living.

Not yet..

I do not believe Jack ever truly loved me, nor do I think he cared much about our children. Jack was nothing more than an immature, greedy alcoholic who worshiped the almighty dollar. The only thing he ever talked about wanting in life was to become rich — but he wanted wealth without putting in any real effort. Jack's favorite pastime was sitting on the couch, getting drunk while watching football. And if there was no football, he would drink and watch any other sport he could find. It didn't matter if there were things around the house that needed fixing — Jack would just lie there like a king on his throne.

For the seven years I lived with Jack after our divorce, he never once treated me with respect or decency. But because he had destroyed my credit and because my self-esteem was so low, I stuck to my seven-year plan: repair the house, rebuild my credit, and restore my sense of self.

I had quietly hoped that somewhere during those seven years, I would meet a man who would inspire me, someone who would help me heal. But that man never came. So instead, I focused all my energy on working full-time, remodeling the house, and raising my son.

By 1996, Joshua was preparing to graduate from high school, and I was so excited. I was proud beyond words that, despite everything, I had managed to raise a happy, healthy, well-adjusted young man. I wanted to throw him a big graduation party — a celebration of everything we had both survived.

But life had other plans.

Less than a week before the party, I found out Joshua would not be graduating with his class. He was short one class credit and would have to attend summer school to make it up.

I was dumbfounded. I couldn't believe it. Joshua had known for weeks but was too afraid to tell me. He knew I had already sent out the graduation invitations. I imagine he didn't know how to face me — or the disappointment he feared he would see in my eyes. And I'm sure he knew how much the humiliation would sting, especially with our family, who had always enjoyed seeing me falter.

My family had spent years teasing and ridiculing me for how I raised Joshua — for loving him too much, for caring too deeply. So when anything went wrong, they took an almost sick pleasure in it. It still breaks my heart to know that.

At first, I considered canceling the party. But I couldn't bring myself to give my mother that satisfaction. So I decided to go ahead with it, pretending everything was fine — not for appearances, but to protect Joshua from the cruel gloating I knew would come if the truth got out.

The party itself was wonderful. Everyone had a good time. But as the evening wound down, panic crept in. That's when I made a desperate, foolish decision: I told everyone that there had been a bomb threat at the school and that the graduation had been postponed.

What was I thinking? I don't know. I just knew I was trying to protect my son from humiliation, trying to save face for both of us.

But, of course, my mother wasn't buying it. She never missed an opportunity to expose me. It wasn't long before my stepfather called. He had contacted the school and learned the truth. The jig was up.

Instead of understanding the place of fear and love I had acted from, my step-siblings cut me off completely. Brian and Connie decided I was beyond forgiveness for trying to shield my son. And my mother gloated.

In August of 1996, Joshua finally graduated. When his name was called, I clapped and cheered with everything I had. Jack, on the other hand, just sat there, silent and expressionless. If it had been a football game, Jack would have been on his feet, screaming and yelling. But when it came to his own son's graduation, he had nothing. That was the moment I realized, once again, that there was something deeply wrong with him.

But that day wasn't about Jack. It was about my son. After the ceremony, we took Joshua out for a nice dinner. I didn't bother telling the rest of the family he had officially graduated. None of them asked anyway.

Now, it was time to prepare Joshua for community college.

At the time, I was working as a case manager for workers' compensation clients at an insurance company just a few miles from our home. The hours and location were perfect. I had the time and energy to help Joshua take the next steps toward adulthood — something my own mother had never done for me. She had thrown me out of the house before I even graduated high school.

Helping Joshua felt healing. We went shopping for new clothes. I helped him with registration. It was a wonderful experience — until it came time for his first report card.

The report card never arrived.

After waiting what felt like forever, I finally asked Joshua about it. He stalled and avoided until, after three weeks, he finally handed it over.

And once again, it was altered — just like his high school report card had been.

I was devastated. Not just by the lying, but by what it said about how lost Joshua was becoming.

I sat him down and told him the truth: I had been willing to give him one year of college to prove that he wanted it. He agreed. But as time went on, it became clear that Joshua's heart wasn't in it. He was drifting.

And so, I made the hard decision. I recommended that he consider joining the armed services. Not because I wanted to send him away, but because I was deeply worried about the direction he was heading — and I knew he needed something bigger than himself to belong to, something that might teach him discipline, purpose, and pride.

Immediately, I informed Joshua that we were going to the recruitment office that he had been a delayed enlistment candidate with the Navy a year prior and I told Joshua that he was now going to enlist. Joshua did not fight about this decision and signed up and was prepared for departure in July of 1997.

So for the next two months, I allowed him to work and to enjoy himself and I did not put any pressure on him because I knew that the change of being a seaman was going to be pretty hard on him. We enjoyed ourselves and had time to relax and just get to know one another. I also knew that having him leave for the Navy was going to break my heart. I wanted Joshua to go to college so badly and to enjoy life like I had wanted and I offered it to him and he did not want it.

July finally arrived, and I knew that the day Joshua would leave home for four years was going to devastate me. I needed to be strong because it was in the best interest of my son to go and to learn what it was that I was failing to teach him.

When the recruiters arrived at 5:00 a.m. on July 2nd, 1997, I was helping Joshua finish up his last-minute packing, trying to remain stoic and not fall apart in front of him. I was also feeling like I had made a terrible mistake. But Joshua was sort of happy and proud to go. I think he was wise enough to know that he needed to go too. The recruiters hurried us up, and then they left.

Joshua promised me that he would telephone as soon as he could and let me know exactly where they had taken him for boot camp. But once that car left and was out of sight, I broke down and cried so hard that I could not even go to work that day. I was so distraught that my cat and my dog stayed by my side the entire day. Animals are just so tuned into their master's emotions, and it is uncanny. I loved both of them so much for their love that day.

I eventually went outside to try and soak up some sun to stop crying, but I just kept on crying and crying from my soul. Then around 3:00 p.m., Joshua came casually walking around the corner like nothing major had happened and said, "Hey Mom." I thought I was hallucinating. Joshua informed me that he had been rejected by the Navy because he had open sores on his big toes and that he needed to have them treated before re-enlisting.

I was in shock, but I was so glad to see him. We spent the next two months having his feet repaired by the podiatrist. Once he received clearance from the podiatrist, he was sent to naval boot camp in Great Lakes, Illinois on October 2nd, 1997. Once again, I was broken-hearted that he had left and that he would be gone for four years, but I had had the time to come to better terms with his leaving, and I vowed to make this time my time and to focus on healing myself.

While Joshua was away, I worked harder than ever to get our dilapidated house ready for sale. I knew that my dog Tasha would be too big to have in a rental, and I knew that my seven-year plan would be ending around the time that her life would be winding down, so I vowed to stay with this regal and loving animal until she passed.

For the next four years, I worked and played with my dog. My dog and my backyard became my solace from a very hostile world. I enjoyed my time with my dog so much. After Joshua had left, we had new neighbors move in next door. They were our age and they also had a Rottweiler, so we had some things in common. We became close friends very quickly. It started out to be fun having next-door neighbors to have fun with and just travel to the next house to play cards, but the fun did not last.

My sister Ruth and her husband started coming over every Sunday to watch football with Jack while I cooked, babysat, and hosted. But Ruth, being an evil person, was sadly going to destroy the good life that I had built by allowing her into my life.

Ruth and the neighbors began to become close friends, and they became so close that they started to disappear from my house while I would be babysitting Ruth's children or cooking our meal — to go and do drugs. They were getting high on Valium, Percocets, Crank, and Crack. I did not notice their absence at first, and I did not realize they were getting high and joking about how they were putting one over on me. But when I did realize it, I asked them to stop. Once I declared that this drug activity would not be tolerated, I was laughed at for being "too uptight" and teased and made fun of, and eventually ostracized by my own sister, her children, and my next-door neighbors.

Since my neighbors and my sister loved to do drugs, my sister and her family just partied next door for the next year. I would ask Jack why that did not bother him, and he would say to just let it roll off my back. I explained to Jack that Ruth told her children that they were barred from coming over to our house anymore — and why was that? Because I would not indulge in the drugs.

Having lost our relationship with our next-door neighbors, being hurt again by my sister, and living in a loveless relationship with Jack, it was too lonely to stay in that situation much longer. I look back on it now and realize that it was probably a good thing, because had it worked out, I might not have ever had the courage to change my life.

For the next three years, I drowned myself in my work, my dog, my house, and anything I could do to help Joshua be successful. I had started working for another insurance company where I could work at home. It was ideal. I was able to be at home and care for my aging dog.

But on August 15th, my dog suddenly became unable to walk. I took her to the veterinarian and was informed that there was nothing further to be done — that Tasha had some sort of debilitating neurological disorder and that she would decline rapidly.

Being a nurse specializing in rehabilitation, I rehabilitated her back to being able to walk on her own. Tasha did really well for the next two months. Then I watched my regal dog of one-hundred and ten pounds fade away to a mere seventy-seven-pound sickly dog, and she eventually became so sick that she was euthanized on November 16th, 2000.

Losing my dog was a great loss. This dog had been my companion for eleven years. She loved me so much, and I loved her so much, but more importantly, I needed her companionship to survive without human love. We had such fun together, and I was at a loss as to how to fill the void of my dog's absence and how I was going to continue living the empty and loveless life I had with Jack and my family.

Because Tasha's death had been heartbreaking to me, Jack did show some empathy and invited me to go with him to Boston for Thanksgiving. At first, I said no to the idea of a trip with Jack to his mother's, but I eventually agreed to go to get away from the sorrow of Tasha's death, and we did end up having a pretty good time. It still was never quite what it should have been had we been friends and lovers, but I made the best of it, and Jack and his family were gracious.

When I returned home from Boston, I began preparing for Christmas because I was so excited that Joshua would be coming home from the Navy to spend two weeks with me. And I knew in my heart that this would be our last Christmas in that house and with Jack and his son. So I wanted to make it the best Christmas that we could have despite the loss of Tasha and the loveless situation.

And I am so glad that I made it nice for everyone — including myself. Our last time together was so grand that it was one of the best Christmases that we ever had in that house — and it was our last. It was also the last Christmas with Jack, Jack Jr., and all of our last Christmases living in Ft. Lauderdale.

Not long after that Christmas, I moved to Hobe Sound, Florida, where I bought a nice little house in a nice neighborhood. I had great expectations when I arrived in Hobe Sound, but I also had great fear of starting over and being all by myself. But I knew that I could not continue on in the situation that I was in and that I wanted an opportunity to have love.

During my first year in Hobe Sound, I met three men in the same month who were around my age and showed significant interest in dating me. I was excited that I was free from Jack, that my son was grown and happy, and that I had a very good job and my own home. It seemed that I had my affairs in order and that now I could meet a man without all of my past baggage and begin to date and enjoy life.

But the fears I had of running into a bad man came true — because all three men turned out to be bad men — and one of them turned out to be a predator. And when I say predator, I do not say that lightly.

The first guy was an alcoholic who preyed on vulnerable women and fairly quickly requested that I liquidate my assets and move with him. While he was awaiting my decision, he began his subtle work of chipping away at my self-esteem. He would tell me that I needed to work out to keep a girlish figure, and he would ogle other women while we were out on dates. He was trying to make me feel like he was as good as I could ever get — that I had better be thankful. Once I recognized his harmful and alcoholic ways, I terminated any contact.

The second guy was just an impaired, hapless, directionless man who smoked marijuana daily and was also an alcoholic. He was fun to date for a few weeks. However, in little over two months, he asked me to marry him.

I knew this man was not good for me and would lead me nowhere good.

I was feeling pretty good that I was able to determine fairly quickly that the first two men were not good for me and would not treat me well. It sort of built up my confidence and shed some of the fear that I wouldn't recognize a bad man.

But my confidence was about to be shattered.

The third guy wasn't just a bad man. He was the scariest of them all — a reflection of two very dangerous and destructive past boyfriends: Tony and Bob. This man was the most damaging type of predator to a susceptible woman.

He was a sociopath — the kind who learns early on about the dynamics of a vulnerable woman's life and then uses that information to control her through torment and fear. Once I realized that this man was the very kind I had always feared meeting, I ended the relationship. But it wasn't over.

Even after I obtained a restraining order, he continued trying to control me through fear, assaults, and intimidation.

At the restraining order hearing, he asked the judge if he could still contact me through his lawyer, and the judge said yes. He then looked over at me and smiled. I knew exactly what that meant because he had told me: if I ever attempted to regain my power and life, he would make my life miserable, sue me, and harass me through every means he could. And he did just that. He sued me — simply because he had the money and the desire to continue controlling me even if he was banned from direct contact.

Once I allowed him into my private thoughts, without realizing the kind of man I was disclosing myself to, I became very vulnerable to his torment. It was exhausting, emotionally and mentally, to rid myself of this human parasite.

Agreeing to start a relationship with such an abusive man shook my self-confidence badly because it showed me that I was still choosing the wrong people due to my emotional damage. I was really upset with myself.

But once I mustered up enough inner strength to get rid of him, I knew what I had to do:

I needed to heal from Jack, Alan, Rich, psycho Tom, and my family.

I made a pact with myself that I would not meet nor date any man for one full year.

It has now been one year since psycho Tom left my life — and it has been a peaceful year.

I took time to write my book, to read, and to think deeply into my psyche. I asked myself to find that wounded inner child and heal her, to carry her through to the present.

Believe me when I tell you: at times, it was so hard to feel the pain.

Now, I understand why people prefer to drug and drink instead of healing.

The pain is unbearable at times — and it is hard work to recover your true self after such traumas, especially without the love of a family.

However, if you do not remain sober, you will constantly repeat the bad choices you made because you are the walking wounded — and predators can smell you coming.

Alcohol or drug intoxication makes you lose your inhibitions and clouds your judgment. You cannot heal the pain of abuse and the mistakes made through a cloudy fog. Healing through sobriety is the only way to truly rid yourself of the past.

If you continue to drink and drug to mask the pain — the pain will NEVER go away. Instead, you will get even more emotionally destroyed, and it will not lead anywhere good.

After recovering from the mistakes I made in choosing husbands and boyfriends, I realize now how dearly those choices cost me. Because of my emotional damage, I chose very harmful people to trust — and they betrayed me for their own unhealthy reasons. Being so damaged made me vulnerable to many mean-spirited people.

Even though I know my past choices were the result of my low self-worth and my pessimistic outlook, those choices could have easily led to my permanent demise had I not had the inner strength to say no to the abuse — and the strong will to survive.

I had been searching for a way out of my misery through a human being or a job — and of course, we know that never works.

I remained very disappointed for a long time about the fact that I never met and married a good, God-fearing man. I wanted to meet and marry someone who would guide me, protect me, and love me. But what I realized, just recently, is that what I was asking for from a man was unhealthy. I wasn't just looking for love — I was asking for parenting because I was never parented. And that kind of neediness turns off a decent man and attracts all the losers, fools, and abusers.

Saying those kinds of key words to a predator is like music to their ears.

I do regret that I have never experienced being part of a loving and nurturing family. But we have to deal with the cards we are dealt — and make the most of it. Believe me when I tell you: I am very sad and I deeply regret that my emotional baggage cost me so much.

To this day, I remain without a loving, nurturing relationship — and I know deep in my heart that real love would have helped me heal faster than anything else.

Starting over in Hobe Sound has been very scary and, at times, very lonely.

After living here for five years, and recovering from psycho Tom, I still felt like I hadn't achieved something important inside myself. I struggled to figure it out.

And then — I finally did figure it out.

What I wanted was to obtain an advanced degree in nursing so that I could teach. I have wanted to teach nursing since 1986.

So, once I recovered from the abusive trauma from psycho Tom, I sold my house and enrolled in college full time, pursuing my advanced nursing degree so I could become a nursing professor. While pursuing my degree, this time out of the workplace and inside academia, it would help me focus on changing my path — and also give back to others through love. Becoming a professor will add so much value to my life. After surviving all that I have survived, I want to begin a new chapter on a positive note — achieving something I have always wanted. Plus, with my twenty-seven years of nursing experience and my background, I know I could bring a lot to the classroom for eager nursing students.

I think I would be a great teacher. I have so much knowledge to share.

What a beautiful way to take the negative that I was given and turn it into a positive.

I have realized that I can't wait for another human being to help heal me.

I have had to do this work all by myself. I have had such anger issues toward men for their abusive treatment of me, and I am very aware that at this time, I am not ready to meet a man who could add love to my life.

Since 2001, I have been single but not available. Now I understand why I didn't meet "Mr. Wonderful" — and it's okay. I needed to focus on ways of improving my overall self.

Putting myself through college to obtain an advanced degree is a pretty good way to feel accomplished and fulfilled. I would rather be single, working in a profession where I am at peace and fulfilled, than living in darkness because I made a bad choice just to have a man in my life. It is simply not worth it.

I need to be emotionally available and healthy before the God-fearing man I once dreamed about is supposed to enter my life.

And as far as my family — today, I do not have a relationship with my mother, because she is still just as sick as she ever was. My father and I tolerate each other, but our relationship remains strained. What saddens me most is that my parents have never apologized. They have never said they were sorry — because they don't even remember what they did to their children.

I used to think that once my parents became older adults, they might finally understand and try to make amends to the two remaining children. But they didn't improve one bit.

My mother runs from her thoughts by staying away from her family, and my father drinks heavily. In a way, I pity them. They never experienced what real love is — not love for a child, not love for themselves. They missed out on the rewards of parenting and loving, because they put nothing into it — and in return, they got nothing back.

Whatever the reasons for their emotional unhealthiness, neither one ever sought God, maturity, sobriety, or love. They never learned throughout their entire lives.

My stepfather is just a shell of a man because of his choice to remain passive to my mother. He never stood up for himself or his children. Because of that, he suffered horrific abuse at her hands, and in turn, it destroyed him and his four children.

My stepmother is struggling with her own life. My sister Ruth is still drugging and drinking. She ran off and married a stranger — and just three months after their marriage, her new husband called me, saying he wanted to send her back home.

What a surprise.

My half-sister Janie does not want to have anything to do with me.

And lastly, my son is finishing up his engineering degree and working as a field engineer in California.

He is very happy in his chosen vocation, and he is doing very well. I believe he has found his place and his peace — and I pray for him every day.

Sometimes, when I look back at how traumatic my life has been in every category, it really shows just how strong my will to survive has been. The odds were truly against me — to make it to a place where I could finally gain understanding, recognize the results of my choices, and learn how to repair the damage.

It took everything I had to gain peace and to start feeling some self-worth, which, in turn, brings personal happiness.

I have to remind myself — it was only by the Grace of God and His Will that I survived it all and now have the strength and courage to share my story with others, with hope for better tomorrows.

I hope I have provided some helpful insight into the chronological abuse that takes place in an abusive home — and how hard the struggle is to survive and overcome it.

I also hope I have given some understanding of why we make such poor choices, and how hard it is to repair the damage of an abusive past without succumbing to addictions.

If you are addicted to a substance, you remain a victim — but you also add another illness.

With an abusive history *and* an addiction, it will eventually destroy you. You will lose yourself. You will snuff out any hope of freeing yourself from the past.

You must stay sober, feel the pain — and you will not die. It is worth it.

Even though my life did not end up as picture-perfect as I once hoped and wished for, I thank God that I survived my tragic childhood and adulthood. I thank God that I survived the abuse from my parents, the rape, the death of my baby brother, the impairment and abuse from my sister, the death of my half-sister, the loss of any relationship with my second half-sister and my stepbrothers and stepsister, and my bad choices of abusive and neglectful friends, husbands, and boyfriends.

Today, I am preparing to go somewhere fun — with the hope that I will experience love and friendship from people who are hopeful, free from their pasts, and who have learned through their journey the value of real love and friendship. It sounds so exciting.

And I plan to arrive at this future place better educated and with far less emotional baggage weighing me down. I feel freer and more alive than I have ever felt.

I am finally doing something that I have always wanted to do. I feel like I have arrived at a peaceful place, with God at my side. Now it is time to live my life completely out of the darkness.

As I contemplate the future with hope and excitement, I can say with peace:

My life is "as good as it gets."

May God and peace be with you.

The End. ◆

BIBLIOGRAPHY

1.   Peck, Scott, M.D. *People of the Lie.*

2.   Stern, Howard. *The Howard Stern Radio Show.*

3.   Clinton, Hillary. Senator, New York.

4.   Winfrey, Oprah. *The Oprah Winfrey Show*, Chicago, IL.

5.   *Family Affair* (Television series).

6.   *Jonathan Livingston Seagull* (Album by Neil Diamond).

7.   The Moody Blues. (1972). Seventh Sojourn [Album]. Threshold Records.

In the midst of every darkness, God's Word remains a guiding light.

JOHN 1:5

"THE LIGHT SHINES
IN THE DARKNESS,
AND THE DARKNESS
HAS NOT OVERCOME
IT."

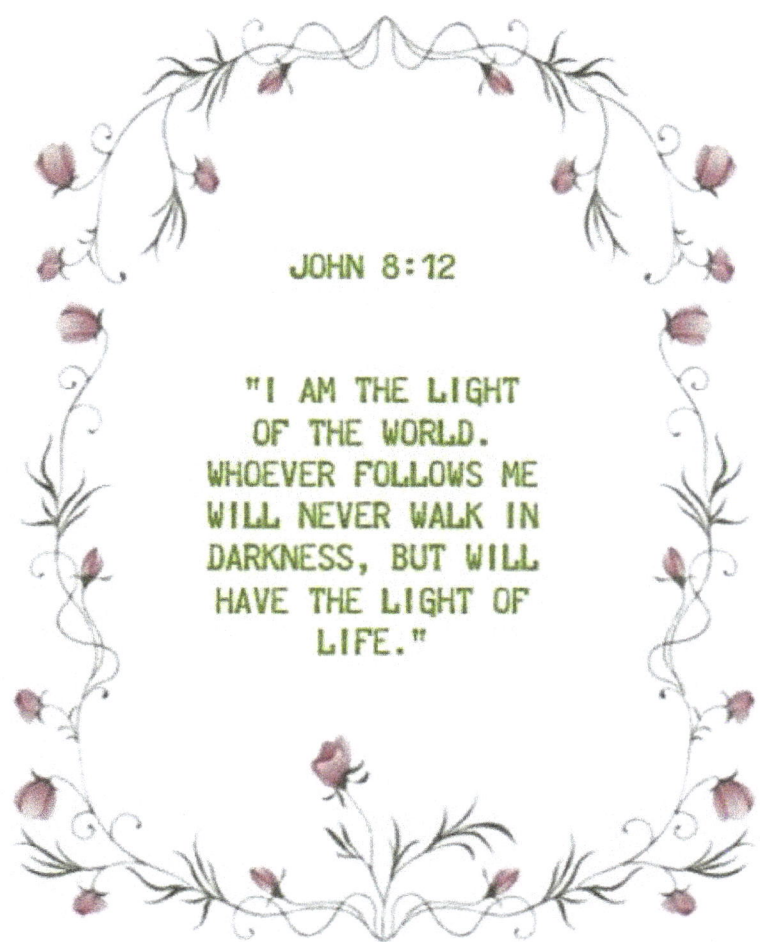

JOHN 8:12

"I AM THE LIGHT
OF THE WORLD.
WHOEVER FOLLOWS ME
WILL NEVER WALK IN
DARKNESS, BUT WILL
HAVE THE LIGHT OF
LIFE."

ABOUT THE AUTHOR

Laura was born in Kentucky and grew up in South Florida. She went to nursing school in North Carolina and received an ADN, RN. Then she finished her nursing degrees at Florida Atlantic University (FAU). She graduated with her Bachelor of Science in Nursing Summa Cum Laude then she completed her Master's Degree. Laura retired from the Department of Veterans Affairs in 2019. Now, she resides in Virginia and works part time as a nurse for the community.

Discover Laura Dunavent's heartfelt narrative on *The Westminster Canterbury Tales* podcast: **Listen here**

To be continued...
"The End of The Line"
was just the beginning.
It started with my father's suicide.
What followed unraveled everything
I thought I knew.
Book Two is coming.

www.ingramcontent.com/pod-product-compliance
Lightning Source LLC
Chambersburg PA
CBHW051143120626
46547CB00012B/920